BBC
WEATHER watch

BBC WEATHER watch

STEPHEN MOSS and
PAUL SIMONS with

The Met. Office

BBC BOOKS

This book is published to accompany the
television series entitled WEATHER WATCH
which was first broadcast in NOVEMBER 1992.
Published by BBC Books,
a division of BBC Enterprises Limited,
Woodlands, 80 Wood Lane,
London W12 0TT

First published 1992
© Stephen Moss, Paul Simons and the British Met. Office 1992

ISBN 0 563 36486 6

Designed by Peartree Design Associates
Edited by Jane Struthers
Picture research by Liz Eddison
Illustrations by Tony Garrett
Set in Plantin Light by Goodfellow & Egan Ltd, Cambridge
Printed and bound in Great Britain by Clays Ltd, St Ives plc
Colour separation by Dot Gradations Ltd, Chelmsford
Cover printed by Clays Ltd, St Ives plc

Contents

Foreword

So you thought the weather was just drizzle and scattered showers? In fact, the British weather is a ferocious beast. Hardly a month goes by without some weather record being broken, from droughts to storms, which is probably why it's an endless topic of conversation and why I'm fascinated by it.

Even our everyday humdrum weather influences the way we live, often in very subtle ways, by affecting the murder and suicide rate, our health, what we eat and drink and even the nation's economy. And small wonder we feel the weather – the natural world is constantly on its guard to changes in weather, with birds, spiders and flowers alert to rain, wind and shine.

Yet although we've been battered by storms, droughts and even little ice ages for thousands of years, the question now is whether our present warmer weather is natural or if we've made it ourselves with our own pollution. We already have a climate warm enough now to grow grapes and make a very decent white wine from them. But on the other hand, global warming could upset the ocean currents like the Gulf Stream that keeps us nice and warm in the winter like a gigantic hot water bottle. If that suddenly changes direction we're going to be left well and truly frozen. Watching the weather really is very important for all our sakes, and this fascinating book will help you enjoy and understand so much more.

Ian McCaskill

Introduction

WHEN TWO FRENCHMEN MEET they talk about love; when two Americans meet they talk about money; when two British people meet they talk about the weather.

The weather is, without doubt, our national obsession. That's hardly surprising: after all, we can have snow in June, warm spells in December and rain all the year round. The British weather can also wield ferocious powers. Tornadoes rip apart buildings, flashfloods devastate towns and thunderstorms contain as much energy as ten Hiroshima bombs. Weirder still, frogs and fish can fall from the sky, and balls of lightning float down the chimney!

Yet even our ordinary, everyday weather exerts a strong influence over the way we live. It affects our mental and physical health, what we eat and drink, and even matters of life and death. Heatwaves and cold snaps vastly increase the death rate, and murder and suicide rates rise during changeable weather conditions. Bad weather has caused battles to be lost, destroyed empires and actually changed the course of world history.

Perhaps strangest of all, hardly a month goes by without another weather record being broken. In the past few years we've experienced some of the most extreme weather since records began, from the worst drought for 250 years to hurricane-force storms causing death and mass destruction. So what on earth is happening to our weather?

Only a few years ago we were told we were heading for another ice age, yet now we're facing fears about global warming. The problem is we still know so little about how the world's weather works. There are historical patterns of weather we simply don't understand. Two hundred years ago the weather turned so cold that the Thames froze and the Scots suffered mass starvation because their harvests were wiped out in what was called the Little Ice Age. Yet in the fourteenth century grapevines were grown as far north as the Pennines. In fact, our climate has always swung from cold to warmth and back again. But now, for the first time in history, *we* seem to be changing the world's climate.

In this book we begin by looking at the wonderful variety of the British weather: extremes like the hottest day, and the wettest place; and freak weather events like giant hailstones. We go on to explain what weather actually is, and how forecasters try to predict what will happen tomorrow, next month and far into the next century. We find out if proverbs hold a grain of truth, and see if we can learn anything from the way plants and animals react to the weather. We see how the weather affects our health, and our wealth.

Finally, we delve into the past, to discover how Britain's weather has influenced our nation's history; and into the future, to learn what sort of weather we can expect in the twenty-first century.

STEPHEN MOSS and PAUL SIMONS

Our Weather

IT'S SOMETIMES SAID that if the sun shines today, it's weather, and if it shines for a year, it's climate. This may be an over-simplification, but it's basically true: when the weather forms a definite pattern over a period of time, you can begin to talk about climate.

Britain's climate is temperate, meaning we rarely experience very hot or very cold temperatures. It is also maritime because of our proximity to the ocean. As a result we experience clear changes in the weather from season to season. Generally, Britain has warm summers, cold (though rarely very cold) winters, and long, coolish, unsettled springs and autumns. It's a climate of variety, not extremes.

Nevertheless, although the average Briton may normally experience a small range of temperatures compared with the resident of Vladivostok, the British climate more than makes up for this in other ways.

UNUSUAL WEATHER CONDITIONS

Perhaps the most famous examples of unusual weather conditions in Britain are the harsh winter of 1962–3, and the long drought of the summer of 1976 and the great storm of October 1987. Each of these events broke new records, and established the weather as the subject of daily conversation, almost to the exclusion of everything else. Each event passed into popular mythology; and just as everyone old enough can remember what they were doing when President Kennedy was shot, so

Above The notorious drought of the summer of 1976 – the longest period without rain for 80 years. Reservoirs like this one at Woodhead Bridge dried up completely, causing severe water shortages in many parts of England and Wales.

Left Eaton Square, in London SW1, after the storm of October 1987. This was the worst storm in south-east England for over 250 years, leaving 19 million trees felled and a £1.5 billion bill for insurance claims.

11

most Britons can recall where they were on Friday 16 October 1987, when the nation awoke to unprecedented devastation.

In fact, although generally the British climate is temperate, there is an astonishing variety in our geographical and seasonal changes, and record temperatures, as the table on the facing page shows.

It's worth noting that the record high and low temperatures both occurred in the last two decades, as did the warmest and coolest summers – indicating that something strange may be happening to our climate, but more of that later (see The Future).

REGIONAL BRITAIN

There are wide regional variations in weather throughout Britain (as you can see from the table on the facing page). While the western and northern side of Britain is drenched in rain, the east and south-east is suffering the worst drought for almost three centuries. On average, Sty Head in the Lake District receives about 4300 mm (170 in) of rain each year, but St Osyth in Essex, roughly 500 km (300 miles) away, only has about 509 mm (20 in). As a rule of thumb, our rainfall tends to increase to the north and west.

Given the relatively small size of Britain, it's surprising how regional our weather is. The key to this variety is our geography. The British Isles lie sandwiched between the north-west edge of the world's largest landmass, Eurasia, and the Atlantic Ocean. So Britain is caught between the extremes of hot and cold weather from the Continent, and warm moist weather from the Atlantic.

Another reason for the range of weather is the variety of our landscape. The west is wetter than the east because of the high land stretching down the west of Britain. As air in Atlantic depressions hits the west side of Britain the air is lifted up over the high land, which increases the rainfall on the windward side of the high land (as shown in the diagram). As the air descends, a 'rain shadow' forms because the air has already dropped much of its water.

The more extreme weather tends to occur in mountainous

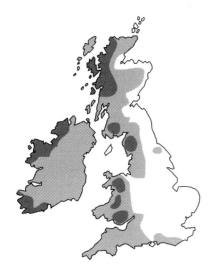

Annual rainfall

 30 inches

60 inches

Rainfall in the British Isles occurs mainly in the west and north, and on higher ground.

12

THE RECORD BREAKERS

Events

Highest temperature
37.1°C (98.8°F)
Cheltenham,
Gloucestershire,
3 August 1990

Lowest temperature
−27.2°C (−17°F)
Braemar, Aberdeenshire,
11 February 1895 and
10 January 1982

Strongest gust of wind
278 kph (173 mph)
Cairngorms, Scotland,
20 March 1986

Heaviest point rainfall
50.8 mm (2 in) in
12 minutes
Wisbech,
Cambridgeshire,
27 June 1970

*Heaviest annual
rainfall*
6528 mm (257 in)
Sprinkling Tarn,
Cumbria, 1954

Places *Mean annual figures*

Warmest place
Isles of Scilly, Cornwall
11.5°C (52.7°F)

Coldest place
Braemar, Aberdeenshire
6.5°C (43.7°F)

Wettest place
Sty Head, Cumbria
4306 mm (169.5 in)

Driest place
St Osyth, Essex
509 mm (20.04 in)

Windiest place
Tiree, Argyllshire
27 kph (17 mph)

Seasons *(England and Wales)*

Warmest summer
1976
Average temperature
17.4°C (63.3°F)

Coolest summer
1981
Average temperature
14.1°C (57.3°F)

Wettest summer
1912
404 mm (15.9 in) of rain

Longest drought
60 days
From 17 March to 15
May 1893, in Sussex

Coldest winter
1963
Average temperature
0.8°C (33.4°F)

Mildest winter
1935 and 1975
Average temperature
6.6°C (43.8°F)

The Cairngorms
Braemar
Tiree
Sprinkling Tarn
Sty Head
Cheltenham
Wisbech
St Osyth

Isles of Scilly

regions where it is often cloudy, wet and windy. The weather in north-west Scotland is particularly severe because of the frequent passage of deep depressions.

The regional patterns for temperature are slightly different. The main factors determining the distribution of temperature are a place's height, latitude and nearness to the coast, particularly the west coast – temperatures are lower inland than near the coast in the winter and warmer inland in the summer. In winter the coldest areas are parts of the Grampian and Tayside regions of Scotland, and the least cold are the extreme south-west of England and the Channel Islands. In July the warmest areas are around London and the coolest are parts of Scotland. Areas near the coast are less warm than inland areas, the opposite to winter, and the temperature decreases from south to north.

South-west and southern England is protected by the warm Atlantic, but on occasions Shrewsbury gets lower temperatures than Kent if the polar Continental airstream sweeps across England. The same applies to hot weather. The hottest air comes off the Continent and so Kent can be hot and dry when everywhere else in Britain is colder. If hot air does travel across Britain it makes places like Cheltenham very hot – the highest official temperature recorded in the United Kingdom was in Cheltenham on 3 August 1990, at 37.1°C (98.8°F).

The western and northern parts of the British Isles also usually lie close to the normal path of the Atlantic depressions. Consequently their winters tend to be mild and stormy while the summers are wet and cool. Overall, the south of the British Isles is usually warmer than the north and the west is wetter than the east. The eastern lowlands of England have a climate similar to that on the Continent (drier, with a wider range of temperature than in the north and west). However, the winters are not as hard as on the Continent.

The severest thunderstorms roar into the south-east of England. Some summer storms start by drawing hot air off the Continental landmass. But they also pick up moisture as they cross the Mediterranean or Bay of Biscay, and as they leave France they only have a short hop across the English Channel before they hit land again and reheat, triggering the thunderstorms. Cornwall also suffers from thunderstorms, especially during the daytime. It's suspected that because Cornwall is a long peninsula with sea on three sides and air moving in from the sea over the land, it has a good feed of moist air for thunderstorms. If conditions are calm the storm stays in one place, which accounts for the most extreme local thunderstorms, such as at Camelford, Lynmouth in 1952 and Martinstown, Dorset on 18 July 1955 (see pages 98–9).

The impact of the weather on the way we live is quite marked. Agriculture on the west side of the country consists more of grasslands and rye which can tolerate wet weather, while the east side grows more cereals, such as oats, barley and wheat which needs less rain. The warmer weather in Kent supports fruit growing while the colder north supports hardier crops such as rye and oats. The south-west is warm and wet, and supports dairy herds and fruit growing in sheltered places. However, the severe drought of the east and south has now brought calls to pump the surplus water of the north and west over to irrigate farmland and replenish the reservoirs in the east and south of Britain.

Other local factors can give rise to unexpected variations in temperature and rainfall for places even a few miles apart. In big cities like London the average temperature is consistently 1–2°C (1.8–3.6°F) warmer than the surrounding countryside. This is because buildings retain heat at night, and because of wasted man-made heat from buildings.

Other odd spots can be found where there are special landscape features. One of the coldest places in Britain is in Rickmansworth, just outside London. Normally as you move up hills the temperature falls, but if it is a good clear night in winter and a location is surrounded by long hill slopes all around then the cold air slides downhill just like water. Rickmansworth sits in amongst the Chilterns and the surrounding cold air spills down into the town and keeps it cold. The locality holds the lowest monthly average temperature in the whole of the United Kingdom, with −8°C (17°F) recorded in December 1935. Such frost hollows are not uncommon.

Parts of southern and eastern England are warm enough to grow grapes for wine-making. This vineyard is at South Kilworth, Leicestershire.

15

Extreme Weather

FOR MOST OF THE TIME British weather is fairly gentle, with a combination of cloud, rain and sun. But don't be deceived. Over the centuries our climate has produced some spectacular and violent surprises, such as devastating storms and floods that have left thousands dead and whole towns obliterated. And the signs are that our weather has taken another turn for the worse in recent times, with some particularly extreme weather.

VIOLENT STORMS

Such ferocious weather is nothing new – the British Isles have been battered by huge gales over many centuries, but there seems little doubt that the worst storm in recorded history was that of 26–27 November 1703. The wind blew at more than hurricane force – 117 kph (73 mph) or more – although, technically speaking, hurricanes can only occur in the tropics. The storm was meticulously documented by Daniel Defoe, author of *Robinson Crusoe*. At about 4 p.m. on 26 November the wind suddenly increased in force with terrific gusts. At least 123 people were killed on land by the storm but losses at sea were far greater: 8000 men were estimated to have drowned. Over 400 windmills were wrecked, some because the intense friction of the rotating blades set their timbers on fire. Over 17 000 trees were blown down in Kent alone. Churches also suffered particularly badly: at least seven lost their steeples. One church spire in Stowmarket, Suffolk, was

blown clean off and sent 8.5 metres (28 feet) down the length of the church before crashing through the roof. The lead on many church roofs was rolled up and carried away by the wind.

Compared to the storm of 1703, how severe was the storm of 1987? The winds which struck south-east England and East Anglia in the early hours of 16 October just about reached hurricane force – blowing at 124 kph (77 mph) – for at least ten minutes at Gorleston in Norfolk and 137 kph (85 mph) at Dover in Kent. Some 3 million households and businesses were left without electricity, 150 000 telephones were cut off and many villages and towns were completely isolated by fallen trees, with 90 per cent of Kent's roads blocked. It's estimated that insurance claims for the night's damage amounted to £1.5 billion – to date, the world's largest insurance claim for a natural disaster. Nineteen people were killed and about 19 million trees were blown down.

The storm in October 1987 was the worst in living memory in southern and eastern England, with winds reaching speeds of up to 137 kph (85 mph) in some places.

What made the storm so strong was the low pressure at its centre and large pressure gradient on its southern flank – the larger the pressure gradient the stronger the wind. The explosive deepening of the low was partly due to an exceptionally large temperature gradient over the Atlantic, and the warm air may have come originally from Hurricane Floyd off the coast of Florida, feeding a depression which deepened into the storm. The other unusual features of the storm were the extremely high temperatures in south-east England during the night, and the enormous pressure rises over southern England to the rear of the low. At Hurn (near Bournemouth) and Heathrow the temperature had been a fairly normal 9°C (48.2°F) at 6 p.m. on the 15th but shot up to 17°C (62.6°F) at midnight. Fears that these temperatures were fuelled by high sea temperatures have highlighted the warnings about the arrival of the greenhouse effect, which is discussed in The Future.

The most recent hurricane-force storm to hit Britain was on Burns Day – 25 January 1990. The storm was in many respects worse than the 1987 one, and affected a greater area of the country. More people were killed (47) because it struck during the daytime. Not as many trees were destroyed as in the 1987 storm, perhaps because they had shed their leaves and so offered less resistance to the wind, and also because their roots were loose in the ground after heavy rains: it is thought that between three and five million trees were lost. Another difference was that the 1990 storm was followed by a month of atrocious weather with frequent gales, sleet, snow and ice and torrential rain.

Even so, how do our hurricane-force storms compare with elsewhere in the world? The most deadly natural disaster in American history was the Galveston Hurricane of 8 September 1900. Early in the day the resort town of Galveston, Texas, was hit by the hurricane and by night-time half the city was underwater with several buildings on the verge of collapse. Wind speeds estimated at over 177 kph (110 mph) sent a 1.5-metre (5-foot) tidal wave through the town. The death toll was estimated at between 10 000 and 12 000.

Gales – which have wind speeds of 62–74 kph (39–46 mph) – are more common in Britain during winter than the summer because depressions are deeper and more vigorous, due to the greater temperature differences that exist between the Equator and the North Pole in winter than in summer: the North Pole is bitterly cold in the winter and less so in the summer.

LIGHTNING

Lightning occurs when static electricity builds up inside a cloud, and is probably created when ice crystals or water droplets violently collide with each other. The base of the cloud collects a small region of positive charge which it has to discharge like a spark jumping a gap, either back into the cloud (sheet lightning) or into the ground (forked lightning). The lightning itself is a sudden shaft of electrical discharge with a high current which may peak at between 10 000 and 40 000 amps.

The lightning flash actually consists of up to 40 zigzag strokes up and down, but they happen so fast that all we see is a flicker. It usually begins with a branching discharge that spreads downward until, at about 100 metres (330 feet) above the ground it pulls up a discharge from the ground. When contact is made, the first return stroke is fired upwards back into the cloud through the ionised channel left in the air by the first strike.

1 Static electricity builds up in a thundercloud so intensely that it has to be discharged, and a leader stroke starts downwards.

2 The leader stroke zigzags to the ground, trying to seek out the easiest path, such as a high point like a tree or building, or a metal object.

3 The leader stroke forms a path for the return stroke – a positive discharge from the ground to the cloud – which gives the flash of lightning. Meanwhile, the intense heating of the air makes it expand rapidly, causing the sonic bang we hear as thunder.

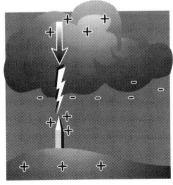

1   2   3

Lightning does strike twice! The Eiffel Tower is a perfect lightning conductor because of its height and metal, and it is struck frequently by lightning, as during this violent storm on 7 June 1992.

Lightning travels at the speed of light – 300 000 kilometres per second (186 000 miles per second) – and is seen virtually instantaneously, but the sound of thunder travels at about 1 kilometre in 3 seconds (1 mile in 5 seconds). So if you see a flash of lightning, then count the seconds before hearing the thunder, you can roughly work out how far away the storm is.

The power of a typical storm is about 1 gigawatt (1 000 000 000 watts), and a small storm about 1 kilometre (0.62 miles) in radius is equivalent in energy to about 10 of the bombs dropped on Hiroshima. The electrical power in a single lightning stroke is about 1 terawatt (1 000 000 000 000 watts), with energy of about 1 gigajoule (1 terawatt in one-thousandth of a second) and the lightning current of up to 250 kiloamps (250 000 amps) may heat the lightning channel to temperatures as high as 30 000°C (86 000°F) – more than the temperature of the sun – in a millisecond or less. This explosive heating causes rapid expansion of the air to produce the sonic bang we call thunder. This hot air expands so rapidly it creates a shock wave, strong enough to throw people who are nearby into the air or even strip off their clothes! This reportedly happened to a group of tourists as they hid under a bush during a thunderstorm at Trento, Italy, in August 1970. They were left naked but, amazingly, uninjured.

It's a myth that lightning never strikes the same place twice. The Empire State Building and the Eiffel Tower are struck on average 20 to 30 times each year, because lightning usually seeks out the highest object, which is why church spires carry lightning conductors. Tall or isolated trees, telegraph poles and exposed hill tops are all dangerous places in a thunderstorm. The frequency with which thunderstorms occur depends upon the landscape and wind patterns. Eastern England experiences more thunder and lightning than most of Britain, with 10 to 20 days of storms per year, but even so there is a narrow strip extending south-west from the Wash, across the Fens and into Leicestershire which rarely experiences storms, although there is no known reason for this.

The effects are varied for those unlucky enough to be struck by lightning, and the Tornado and Storm Research Organisa-

WHAT TO DO IN A THUNDERSTORM

When lightning strikes the ground there is an enormous voltage on the surface as the current seeps away. It is short-lived but can produce several thousand volts between the feet of nearby people – the wider the space, the greater the current. Here are some of TORRO's guidelines for avoiding injury in a storm.

Avoid animals, lying on the ground or standing with legs apart.

Avoid holding an umbrella or any other metal object.

Avoid wide open spaces and tall or isolated trees or poles.

Shelter in a car with the windows wound up and the doors closed.

Stay inside a building and shut all the windows and doors.

Keep feet together and crouch low with hands on knees.

tion (TORRO) has collected reports of people being blown up, cooked from their insides outwards, or left with marks or holes after being punctured by lightning. Lightning also strikes metal objects, such as umbrellas, golf clubs, telephones or even tea strainers. Lightning struck through the window of the home of a woman in Maidenhead, Berkshire, in July 1982. She was holding a steel tea strainer near an open window when a bolt of lightning struck the strainer. She was hurled across the kitchen but suffered only shock. Jayne Bradshaw, of Stannington, near Sheffield, telephoned her husband during a violent thunderstorm in August 1988. Suddenly there was a noise and she felt a loud bang in her ear. Lightning had struck the telephone wires and passed through her body. She was treated for shock and for burns on her ear and thigh.

Golfers are particularly prone to lightning strikes. One of the most famous incidents was during the Western Open in Chicago on 27 June 1975. Lee Trevino was sitting on the edge of a green by a lake waiting for a shower to pass. Suddenly, lightning threw him into the air and he blacked out. Trevino was taken to hospital with four burn marks on his shoulder where the lightning had left his body. Evidently the lightning had flashed off the lake, shot through the metal shafts of his golf club and passed up his back. Although his back continued to give pain for several years he did return to form.

Lightning causes fatalities, injuries and damage, but it does have the beneficial effect of replenishing the earth with nitrogen. The heat of the lightning flash produces nitrous oxides which are washed down and fertilise the soil – 100 million tonnes of nitrogen are returned each year.

HAILSTORMS

The most severe recorded hailstorm in Britain was probably the one which struck Hitchin and Offley in Hertfordshire on 15 May 1697. The hailstones were about 60 mm (2¼ in) in diameter in Hitchin and 110 mm (4¼ in) in Offley, with some reputed to be 140 mm (5½ in). There was at least one death, the ground was torn up and great oak trees split in two.

The biggest hailstone in the world weighed 0.6 kg (1½ lb) and fell in Coffeyville in Kansas on 3 September 1970. Isolated iceblocks have been recorded throughout history and they can be extraordinarily large. On 2 April 1973, a storm struck Manchester while Dr R F Griffiths, a postgraduate at Manchester University, was walking along the road. He and many other witnesses saw a single flash of lightning of unusual intensity, while a few miles away hail fell. A short while later Dr Griffiths saw an enormous chunk of ice crash and shatter on to the road in front of him. He collected the largest piece of ice – it measured 13.9 cm (5½ in) and weighed 623.6 g (22 oz), although it was only about a third of the original block of ice that had fallen. Further analysis showed it was highly unlikely to have fallen off an aircraft. It bore many similarities to hail, although its crystals were much larger and its layers of ice much more regular.

Perhaps the most spectacular recorded example of an ice chunk falling from the sky was at Ord in Ross-shire on the evening of 13 August 1849 – it was about 6 metres (20 feet) across. *The Times* reported that it had a beautiful crystalline appearance and was almost transparent.

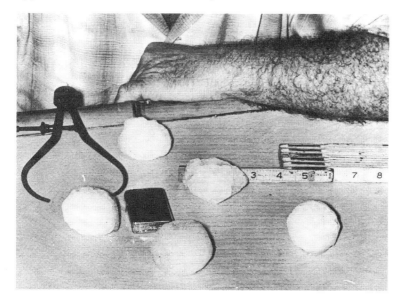

These giant hailstones, measuring 6.9 cm (2¾ in) across, fell at Daytona Beach, Florida, on 30 March 1960, during a hailstorm that covered more than 40 kilometres (25 miles) of coastline.

The East Coast floods of January 1953 cost 300 lives. But sea defences along the coast are once again in a poor state – might the floods happen again?

DELUGES

The record deluge in Britain took place at Martinstown, near Dorchester in Dorset, on 18 July 1955, when 279 mm (11 in) of rain fell during a 15-hour storm. This is a sizeable downpour – the average rainfall of London is 609 mm (24 in) per year. But even more intense rainfalls occur in a shorter time and cause severe flooding. For instance, on 5 August 1981, 43 mm (1¾ in) fell on Manchester Airport and the next day 71 mm (2¾ in) fell on Crouch End in London. The damage varies widely: at Martinstown the flooding was not severe because the underlying chalk absorbed most of the rainwater. However, on 15 August 1952, 250 mm (9¾ in) of rain fell in 12 hours at Lynmouth in North Devon and triggered floods which caused 34 deaths and destroyed the town. Built-up areas are more prone to severe rainstorms because they give off more heat. North-west London had a remarkable slow-moving rainstorm on 14 August 1975 when 171 mm (6¾ in) of rain fell in about 3 hours at Hampstead, drowning one man, flooding 100 homes and causing damage estimated at over £1 million. Yet the London Weather Centre just 3.2 kilometres (2 miles) away had only 5 mm (¼ in) of rain.

FLOODS

The British Isles have suffered great numbers of floods. On 31 January 1953 disastrous floods struck eastern England and the Netherlands, with 1800 lives lost on the Continent and about 300 in Britain. High tides had clashed with a storm surge to drive the water over the top of sea defences along the east coast. This type of flooding is almost equivalent to the abnormally high tides and gales caused by tropical storms.

What, then, are the chances of London flooding? If the North Sea is driven by northerly gale force winds down into the shallow basin of the Straits of Dover it sloshes against the Dutch coast like water in a bath and then surges back into the Thames estuary. If that coincides with a high tide then the water could move up the Thames and flood London. It was this possibility that prompted the building of the Thames flood barrier at Woolwich to prevent London flooding.

THE 1976 DROUGHT

Anyone old enough to remember T Rex, Slade and the last Labour government will also recall the long hot summer of 1976. As Britain sweltered under the merciless gaze of the sun, no one escaped the heat. Reservoirs and rivers dried up, roads melted, and Guardsmen on duty at Buckingham Palace passed out in their hot uniforms. The *Daily Mirror* newspaper summed it up with one of its most famous headlines, 'Phew! What a scorcher!'

Yet while the country was enjoying non-stop conversation about the weather, the drought was having serious repercussions. Water supplies soon ran out in many parts of southern England, and over one million people were forced to collect their water from standpipes in the street. As the summer continued, elderly people suffered strokes and heart attacks brought on by the interminable heat. Trees, deprived of essential water, extended their roots deep into the soil and damaged the foundations of houses.

So what made 1976 different from the traditional damp British summer? Well, in normal summers the British weather follows a familiar pattern. High pressure areas bring periods of settled weather. Occasionally these are displaced by areas of low pressure, bringing much-needed rain to gardens and farms and causing the familiar sight of the covers going on to the Wimbledon tennis courts.

But in the early summer of 1976, something strange happened. Instead of drifting off towards Scandinavia after a few days, the high pressure area over the British Isles simply stuck there – while the depressions moved round the edges. This phenomenon, known as a 'blocking anticyclone', had the knock-on effect of bringing heavy rain to the normally dry and sunny Mediterranean area.

At first, Britain enjoyed the typical benefits of high pressure: warm, dry, settled weather. However, as the month of June wore on, a 'pressure-cooker' effect built up, with the nights getting warmer and warmer, and the days becoming hotter and hotter.

During June and July 1976, the temperature continued to

rise inexorably. From 25 June the temperature reached above 32°C (89.6°F) somewhere in Britain every day for two weeks. The peak was 35°C (95°F), just short of the all-time British record. On St Swithin's Day (15 July) a desperate government passed the United Kingdom's first ever Drought Bill and, to the accompaniment of much derision in the popular press, appointed the luckless Denis Howell as Minister for Drought. The bill gave wide powers to local authorities, enabling them to pass heavy fines on people caught wasting water. Throughout the suburbs of Britain, lawns were cracked and bleached brown and bare, and cherished plants gave up the ghost and died. Still, the heatwave continued. By August, many parts of England and Wales had experienced as much as 35–40 days without rain.

Then, as Britain prepared for the August Bank Holiday, the high pressure system which had dominated the summer's weather for so long finally began to retreat. As it did so, the depressions moved in with a vengeance, bringing downpours over a wide area of England and Wales, and ruining the Bank Holiday for many people! Ironically, the following month was the second wettest September this century, causing widespread floods.

The 1976 drought wasn't the longest period without rain – that dubious honour belongs to a localised drought during 1893. What made the 1976 drought the worst since records began was that it affected such a wide area of the country for so long. Overall, 1975 and 1976 produced the driest 12-month and 18-month periods in England and Wales since early in the nineteenth century.

One of the reasons the drought was so serious was that the previous year, 1975, was itself the fifth driest this century, leaving rivers and reservoirs at dangerously low levels.

Previous notable droughts included the years 1665–6, which culminated in the tinder-dry wooden buildings of London being destroyed in the Great Fire, on 2 September 1666. Thousands of houses and public buildings, including St Paul's Cathedral, were completely destroyed.

The damage caused by the 1976 drought wasn't quite so

spectacular, but in many ways it was more far-reaching in its effects. The British farming industry lost crops with an estimated value of £500 million. Grass dried out, milk yields fell and lambs took longer to fatten. As the soil dried out and cracked, root crops were badly affected and vegetable prices rose. Thousands of acres of forest were lost to fire, which caused £1 million worth of damage in Devon alone. Flora and fauna were badly affected, too. The shortage of water robbed older trees of their strength, which helped the spread of the notorious Dutch Elm Disease.

Since summer 1976 we haven't experienced the same concentrated period without rain. Yet today we are suffering the effects of a longer and potentially more serious drought. During the 1980s eastern and southern parts of Britain experienced a series of hot, dry summers following dry winters. As a result, rivers, reservoirs and underground aquifers are drying out, leading to permanent hosepipe bans over much of East Anglia and southern England. What's more, the drought shows no signs of ending: Met. Office records show that during the late 1980s the rainfall in southeast England was consistently below average, and that during the winter of 1991–2 the region received only one-third of the expected amount of rain. Ironically, the north and west of Britain is still drenched with rain and has plenty of surplus water, but the cost of carrying it down to the drought-stricken regions is prohibitively expensive.

What deep water? This is the Milton Keynes reservoir during the summer of 1976.

A car covered in Saharan sand. Sand is carried over from North Africa by low pressure systems, something which happens more frequently than you might expect.

SAHARAN SAND

On 1 July 1968 a low pressure system moved up over North Africa and Spain and brought a temperature of 32°C (89.6°F) for London and 34°C (93.2°F) at Liphook in Hampshire. The most remarkable feature of this heatwave was a thick deposit of fine reddish dust covering a wide area of the south of England and the Midlands. This was Saharan sand carried up in sandstorms and sent aloft in the hot air.

Saharan dust arrives in Britain about two or three times a year on average. Usually a pale beige covering lies unnoticed after a rainfall. It generally travels the 2600 kilometres (1600 miles) to Britain on a strong southerly wind in about two days. As the dust reaches Britain it can get washed down from rain-bearing clouds, and thousands of tonnes are deposited on the ground.

COLD SPELLS

The record low temperature for the British Isles is −27.2°C (−17°F) at Braemar in Scotland on 11 February 1895 and again on 10 January 1982. In fact, the whole of Britain was bitterly cold in early 1982: Shawbury in Shropshire came close to the British record. To put our cold weather into perspective, however, the world record is −89.2°C (−128.6°F) at the Vostok base in Antarctica, and Canadian and Siberian sites are frequently below the British all-time record.

In winter, low temperatures occur when there are clear skies overnight. Without cloud cover, which acts like a blanket, the heat from the ground escapes upwards. Calm weather conditions allow the air to be cooled near the ground, and because the nights are long in winter they allow more cooling – the further north the location, the longer the nights and the more cooling that takes place.

The four coldest winters in Britain this century (in order of coldness) were 1962–3, 1946–7, 1939–40 and 1916–17. In 1947 Britain was struggling to recover from the shortages and deprivations of wartime. Coal supplies to power stations were held up on the frozen railways, and so electricity restrictions were introduced in early February with domestic supplies cut

off for up to five hours a day. The effects on industry were disastrous: workers had to be laid off temporarily with the result that unemployment reached 2 million for a short time and production fell by 25 per cent. Many people blamed the Labour government for exacerbating the crisis, having nationalised the coal industry a short while before. Some historians even pin this blame on the downfall of Labour at the following general election in 1950, when their majority was cut to six.

The impact of the prolonged 1962–3 severe winter was less dramatic, since the economy and energy supplies were in better shape. Even so, economic activity still dropped by about 7 per cent and unemployment increased with 160 000 workers laid off. At least 49 people were also killed by the direct effects of the severe weather.

The bitter winter of 1962–3 was the coldest this century. In some places the snow lay continuously on the ground from Boxing Day until April. Transport services came to a halt, as here at Lenham, Kent, in January 1963.

Weather Freaks

ACCORDING TO *The Times* of 24 September 1973, tens of thousands of small toads fell from the sky the previous day in a 'freak storm' on to the French village of Brignoles. *The Times* blamed it on recent tornadoes.

It seems utterly bizarre, but *The Times* report is not so very unusual. Showers of toads and frogs have been recorded since the days of Pliny. They mostly appear to consist of local showers of young toads or frogs, usually living and seen to fall from the sky during rainfall. Britain has been blessed with a bewildering variety of strange showers of foreign objects: flounder and smelt fish (east London, 1984), sticklebacks, newts and tadpoles (Rayleigh, Essex, 1930 or 1931), periwinkles and starfish (Thirsk, Yorkshire, 1984), young eels (Oxfordshire, 1960s) and many more.

MANNA FROM HEAVEN?

When the Children of Israel collected manna from Heaven during their exodus from Egypt, did they experience a miracle? There's been a surprising amount of controversy about the subject, given that the accounts of the phenomenon are somewhat old. Some say the manna was sticky sweet sap oozing out of the tamarisk, a shrub growing in the Wadi Feiron where the Israelites are believed to have camped. On the other hand, there could be a meteorological explanation.

Showers of nutritious lichen are known to occur in the Middle East. *Leconora esculenta* is a rather flaky lichen which

easily peels off the rocks on which it grows and rolls around in the wind. There are several cases of people being showered with it and then eating it. For instance, in 1829 during the war between Prussia and Russia, there was severe famine in a large part of the region around the Caspian Sea. One day, during a violent wind, the surface of the countryside became covered in the lichen, which witnesses claimed 'fell down from Heaven'. Seeing their sheep happily eating it, the locals ground down the lichen into flour and made bread from it.

There are other possible types of manna, but what causes it is a mystery. On 13 March 1977, as Alfred Osborne and his wife were returning home from a church service they heard a clicking noise. Suddenly hundreds of nuts fell down from a practically clear sky, bouncing off cars (as reported in the *Bristol Evening Post* on 14 March 1977). It's even more puzzling where fresh ripe hazelnuts could come from in mid-March, as they don't mature in Britain until late summer.

Even stranger is the story of Roland Moody of Southampton, who was in his conservatory on the morning of 12 February 1979. He heard a rushing sound on the glass roof and looked up to see a cascade of seeds hitting the house and garden. The seeds were mustard and cress, but later that day five or six more falls followed, including maize, peas and bean seeds. The seeds later germinated into proper plants. Possibly the most exotic form of manna to fall to earth was a shower of meat over the backyard of a house, reported in Kentucky in 1876. The local newspaper, *Bath County News*, wrote 'Mrs Crouch was out in the yard at the time making soap, when meat which looked like beef began to fall around her. The sky was perfectly clear at the time, and she said it fell like large snowflakes.' The meat was apparently perfectly fresh and tasted of either mutton or venison.

Heaven knows what the Israelites really found in the wilderness, but they may have had a pretty good menu to choose from.

The current popular explanation of all these weird showers points to waterspouts, which scoop up frogs or fishes from lakes or seas, carry them for miles and dump them on land.

Delighted Israelites collect manna falling from Heaven. It may have been a species of lichen carried into the air by strong winds.

But why aren't the creatures rained down with the rest of their habitat – stones, rocks, weeds or other animals? Perhaps the vortex of a tornado or waterspout and the thundercloud above it would drop materials too small or large for it to carry.

TORNADOES

If all of this smacks of something cranky, it's worth considering the effect of tornadoes. Southern England lies at the edge of a tornado zone stretching across Europe. We have between 20 and 60 tornadoes each year, mostly with wind speeds of about 117–183 kph (73–114 mph), roughly the same speed as the 1987 storm. Unlike hurricane-force storms, tornadoes consist of columns of rapidly rotating air that look like funnels and so strike a very narrow area (usually about 100 metres [110 yards] in diameter), although the worst British cases are as severe as the average North American ones.

Severe tornadoes with wind speeds of 290 kph (180 mph) have been recorded 28 times this century in south, central and eastern England. The worst ones of up to 341 kph (212 mph) have resulted in three devastating tornadoes this century, including one that hit west London during the afternoon rush hour on 8 December 1954. The tornado ripped a track about 90–365 metres (100–400 yards) wide for 15 kilometres (9 miles) through Chiswick, Gunnersbury, Acton, Golders Green and Southgate. Gunnersbury railway station lost its roof and six people were injured. A factory at Acton was destroyed and 12 people there were injured. As an eye-witness in Acton reported, 'I saw a car flying by my shop 15 feet in the air. It landed upright without bursting a tyre.'

The United States suffers the worst tornado disasters. Each year it is hit by around 1000 tornadoes, and an average of 89 people are killed. The most devastating one in recorded American history occurred on 18 March 1925. At 1 p.m. a huge thunderstorm cloud developed a vortex at the front of the cloud near Ellington in south-east Missouri. A quarter of an hour later it struck Annapolis, Missouri, and then headed north-east in a straight line, travelling at 96 kph (60 mph) to Illinois where it completely destroyed the town of Gorham. On

Facing page Tornadoes are often created in thunderstorms when warm moist air is sucked up into the cloud and rubs against a cold down-draught. The air caught in between spins rather like a top, starting a whirlpool of wind that slowly extends down to the ground. Once it reaches the ground the intense low pressure inside the tornado acts like a vacuum cleaner, sucking up anything in its path, while the violent winds spinning round the edge pulverise buildings, trees and other objects.

its way its width grew from 0.4 kilometre (¼ mile) to nearly 1.6 kilometres (1 mile). This enormous funnel looked like a monstrous inverted cone, truncated at the ground, with lightning darting through it and accompanied by a constant thundering roar like a giant freight train. The winds were so strong that bodies were thrown 2.4 kilometres (1½ miles) out of town.

The tornado then picked up speed and crossed into Indiana, completely destroying the town of Griffin, and then ripped up a quarter of Princeton before finally dissipating. It had been active for 3½ hours, during which time it left a trail of devastation along 350 kilometres (220 miles), killing 689 and injuring 1980 people, destroying four towns, severely damaging six others and leaving 11 000 homeless.

Tornadoes are often created inside a thunderstorm as air is sucked upwards and rubs against air already passing upwards. The rubbing makes the air spin and forms the tornado. The funnel of air spins down to the ground and then spins in a vortex, sucking in more air from its surroundings. The damage to buildings is caused by the tornado's strong winds lifting roofs and pushing out walls. Objects in the houses can also be sucked through open windows, up chimneys, and through other openings in the buildings. If the spout of spinning air hits water it sucks it up into a waterspout, which may explain the reports of fish and other animals being carried far inland and then dumped from a great height.

Prehistoric monuments may also be linked with tornadoes. Tornadoes tend to pass in certain directions and Dr Terence Meaden of TORRO has discovered that prehistoric causeways, known as cursuses, at stone circles tend to point in the same directions. Each cursus is about the same shape, length and width as the track of a severe tornado, such as the 2.7-kilometre (1½-mile) Stonehenge cursus which runs past Stonehenge itself. It's possible that severe tornadoes, with their roaring sound, sweeping damage and sometimes hail and lightning, might have been seen as religious signs or phenomena by prehistoric societies and later commemorated in their stone circles.

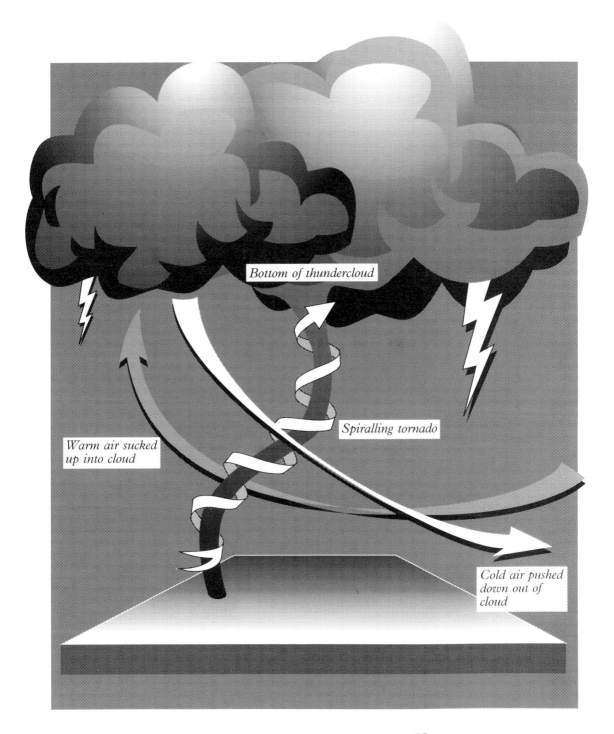

Bottom of thundercloud

Spiralling tornado

Warm air sucked
up into cloud

Cold air pushed
down out of
cloud

CORN CIRCLES

Dr Meaden has also been collecting reports about corn circles, the flattened circles of cereal crops which appear during the summer. He has surveyed over 150 corn circles since 1980 and suggests that they are formed by a sort of whirlwind. A spiral vortex of air – invisible to the eye – could be formed by narrow descending eddy currents, plunging down when a wind passes over a hill. Meaden describes these vortices as 'atmospheric whirlpools'. Unfortunately this genuinely scientific investigation has attracted hoaxers who have made their own artificial corn circles and helped to discredit the *bona fide* scientists.

Hoaxes, extra-terrestrial messages or meteorological marvels? Corn circles like this one at Headbourne Worthy, near Winchester, may be the result of freak whirlwinds.

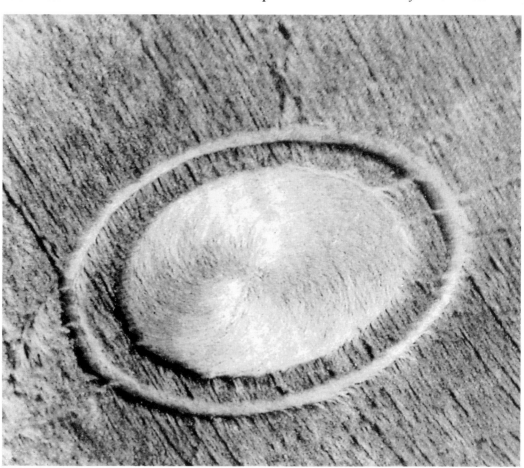

BALL LIGHTNING

There have been reports going back thousands of years of mysterious glowing balls of light hovering or slowly passing through the air. The glowing balls vary from the size of a grapefruit to a football, and can float around houses or vehicles after lightning storms. Take this report by the Soviet news agency TASS of a ball of lightning inside an aircraft on a flight across the Soviet Union. The ball was 10 cm (4 in) across, and appeared on the fuselage in front of the cockpit of an Ilyushin-18 aircraft as it flew close to a thunderstorm over the Black Sea on 15 January 1984.

'It disappeared with a deafening noise, but re-emerged several seconds later in the passengers' lounge, after piercing in an uncanny way through the air-tight metal wall' reported TASS. 'The fireball slowly flew above the heads of the stunned passengers. In the tail section of the airliner it divided into two glowing crescents which then joined together again and left the plane almost noiselessly'.

The radar and other instruments aboard the plane were damaged, and two holes were found in the fuselage, but no passengers were hurt during the episode.

Ball lightning also has an attraction for other closed spaces, such as houses, which it enters through an open window or door, the chimney and sometimes even through small cracks, frequently entering kitchens from the fireplace. Take this description by Arthur Covington reported in the science magazine *Nature* on 18 April 1970: 'We saw a ball of light emerge from the fireplace and slowly drift across the room. It appeared to pass through a curtained, closed window without making any noise or causing any damage. A loud detonation was heard a few moments after the ball vanished.'

Ball lightning is usually reported during a thunderstorm, often a particularly violent one (although there are also reports of ball lightning associated with tornadoes and even earthquakes or volcanoes). The most convincing explanation is that it is an electrostatic phenomenon, and recent laboratory experiments have backed up this theory by re-creating something like natural ball lightning.

What makes the Weather?

THE WEATHER AT ANY PARTICULAR PLACE depends on three ingredients, and it is the mixture of these ingredients around the world that creates all our weather. They are: the heat from the sun; the wind (which is really just the motion of the air); the water in the air in the form of gas (called water vapour) or water droplets.

The sun is the driving force behind the weather. It heats up the earth, but not evenly. Because the earth is a sphere, the sun's heating action is spread over a larger area at the poles than in the tropics. This means the poles are much colder than the tropics. The temperature of any place in the world is mainly determined by its distance from the Equator.

The sun is also responsible for the wind, because it heats up the earth, which in turn heats up the air. In the tropics the air is gaining more heat from the sun than is being lost, while the opposite happens at the poles. In theory, this could cause the tropics to get hotter and the poles colder and colder, but in reality that does not happen because the winds take heat from the tropics to the poles. Hot air rises at the Equator and heads towards the poles high up in the atmosphere. At the same time cold air sinks at the poles and travels towards the Equator at the surface (as shown in the diagram on the facing page). However, because the earth is spinning, the winds are more complicated than this.

There is water vapour in the air, partly caused by the sun evaporating water from the sea. If the air is rising, the

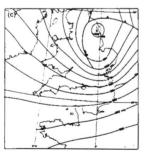

A weather chart illustrating the storm of October 1987. The tightly packed isobars indicate the strength of the wind.

temperature of the air decreases and the air reaches the stage where it cannot hold the water vapour. When this happens the vapour condenses into water droplets which make clouds, and when the droplets of water become large enough they fall as rain. Areas of rising air are associated with low pressure (also known as depressions). In general, low pressure areas are associated with cloud and rain, and generally unsettled weather. On the other hand, in high pressure areas (also known as anticyclones), the air sinks, and so becomes warmer and drier, which inhibits the formation of clouds. In high pressure areas the weather is usually dry, and often sunny and settled. You can now understand why meteorologists love talking about areas of low pressure and high pressure in weather forecasts.

The importance of air pressure can't be stressed too much. The trouble is, it's difficult to appreciate air pressure because we're usually unaware of it. You can feel it going up or down in a lift, car or plane, but the differences in the pressures in the weather are minute in comparison. A fall of surface pressure of just 2 millibars from 1004 to 1002 in one hour is quite dramatic in weather terms and would usually occur when a depression is approaching quite quickly.

To meteorologists the weather chart of highs and lows is the basic working tool (see the diagram on the facing page). The familiar isobars are simply lines joining places with the same surface pressure. From the isobars you can measure the wind speed and direction – the wind flows along the isobars, and the more tightly packed the isobars the stronger the wind. An understanding of the pressure patterns gives you the starting point for the predictions of cloud, rain and temperature. Hence the obsession with pressure patterns.

BRITISH WEATHER: THE BATTLE OF HOT VERSUS COLD

So how does this affect our weather in Britain? We're in rather an odd situation, halfway between the Equator and the poles in a battle zone between hot and cold air. We get cold polar air as it rushes south towards the Equator, and sometimes we get warm tropical air as it travels north towards the Arctic (as

The planet's winds follow a very simple rule: warm air rises, cold air sinks. Because the earth is a sphere, air is warmed more at the Equator than at the poles, and this hot air expands and forces the air already aloft towards the poles, where the air has cooled, descended and forced the lower air towards the tropics again.

The rotation of the earth bends the winds into patterns, with trade winds in the tropics blowing from the north-east in the northern hemisphere and from the south-east in the southern hemisphere.

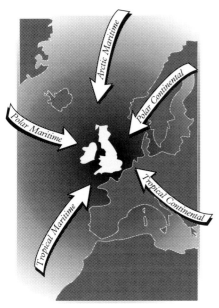

Britain is blessed with a wonderful variety of weather that comes at us from all sorts of places. Air masses from the icy Arctic leave us shivering and sometimes snowy, but when tropical continental air blows in during the summer we usually have hot, dry, sunny weather. Polar continental air originates over Siberia and is very cold and fairly dry. More often our winter weather comes from air masses from the west – polar maritime air usually comes from Greenland and is relatively cold. Tropical maritime winds keep us fairly cool in the summer but warm in the winter.

shown in the diagram). But Britain is also sandwiched between the warmth of the Atlantic Gulf Stream and the extreme heat or cold of continental Europe, and it is partly thanks to these different airstreams that the British climate is blessed with a variety of weather; small wonder the weather is the staple topic of British conversation.

DEPRESSIONS

Most of Britain's weather comes from the west, as depressions sweep in off the Atlantic. Every depression has its own life story, but here is a typical outline. Depressions are created by atmospheric warfare. When cold polar air from the north and warm tropical air from the south meet they form a front (a name coined after the First World War battle fronts, which is apt considering the dramatic weather that can be formed on the front). Fronts often form in the North Atlantic in winter when the cold air blowing off the eastern United States hits warmer air which has come off the Gulf Stream. As a result, a belt of cloud and rain usually exists along the length of the front.

However, the battle between the warm and cold air creates different types of fronts. As the two colossal air masses struggle with each other the front starts rippling, sometimes developing into waves. The warm air gets the upper hand at the leading edge of the wave and pushes back the cold air – this is the warm front. Meanwhile, at the trailing edge of the wave the cold air drives back the warm air – this is the cold front. Imagine it as two sumo wrestlers slogging it out, with the warm air pushing forward while the cold air pushes from behind. And where the warm and cold fronts meet a depression forms.

By now the depression will look like the familiar satellite pictures you see on television weather forecasts, with clouds swirling around a low pressure centre where the air is rising. On a weather map the isobars are centred around the low pressure labelled 'L', a warm front is shown as a red line with semi-circles and a cold front shown as a blue line with triangles.

Meanwhile, the depression is guided eastwards and north-wards by jet stream winds high up in the atmosphere, heading towards Scotland and Scandinavia. Worse still for the Scots and Scandinavians, as the depression travels across the Atlantic it picks up more moisture from the sea, which will eventually fall as rain or snow. The depression can also strengthen (known as 'deepening'). Thanks to the jet stream high above, more air flows upwards and outwards than is replaced at the surface, so the pressure falls. The lower it falls the closer together the isobars become and the windier it is, sometimes developing into a full-blown storm like that of 15–16 October 1987 and 25 January 1990 (see Extreme Weather). But take heart: usually a winter depression just brings us wind, rain and warm air and very often it has gone through its complete life cycle before it even reaches our shores.

A satellite picture, taken on 16 October 1987, showing the storm moving across the British Isles.

WARM AND COLD FRONTS

Let's look again at the warm front. Warm air tries to push the cool air out of its way, but the cool air is denser and forces the warm air to ride up over it in a gradual slope. As the warm moist air is forced upwards it cools, condensing the water vapour in the air into droplets, creating clouds.

This is what it looks like on the ground as a typical warm front approaches. Six to twelve hours before the warm front arrives the wind blows from the south-west and you can see typical cirrus 'mare's tail' clouds high up, followed by a lower flat grey veil of altostratus clouds gradually blocking out the sun. The clouds get lower and lower and rain becomes heavier and more persistent as the front approaches. Eventually the front itself arrives, and the rain eases and usually turns to drizzle. The wind swings more westerly and warmer air follows. The weather is generally mild and cloudy, sometimes with drizzle, although in summer the sky is clear.

The cold front gives much shorter warning of its approach. It is often obscured by low cloud in the preceding warm air, but is more violent than the warm front because the cold air is denser and rams the warm air up into a steep climb, producing more spectacular weather. Viewed from the ground you can see a narrow band of thick black rain-bearing clouds (nimbo-

41

THE LIFE STORY OF A DEPRESSION

The diagrams on these two pages illustrate the life of a depression. In each case, the top illustration shows what is taking place in the sky, and the bottom one shows what you would see on a weather map.

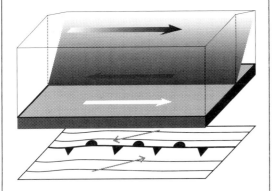

1 A depression begins with a 'battle' between warm air from the tropics and cold air from the poles. There is friction between the winds.

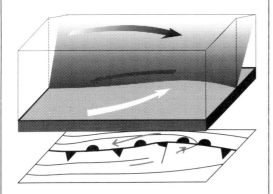

2 The friction causes ripples on the front. Occasionally one of these will start to grow into a wave.

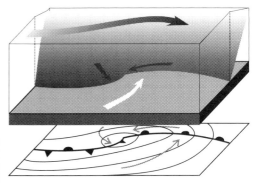

3 Near the tip of the wave the front bends into warm and cold fronts – the warm front is shown as a line with semi-circles and the cold front as a line with triangles. These diagrams exaggerate the steepness of the fronts. The average warm frontal slope is 1:150 and the cold front is 1:50.

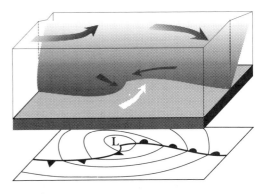

4 At the warm front (the line with semi-circles), the warm air slowly rises over the cold, making a wide bank of cloud. But things are more dramatic on the cold front. The warm air is thrust into a steep slope high up into the sky, making a thin wedge of big clouds, sometimes with the most violent of all clouds (the cumulonimbus thunderclouds), and on rare occasions accompanied by tornadoes.

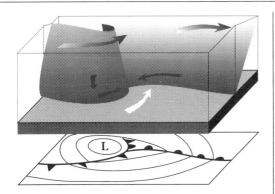

5 Meanwhile, in the middle of the depression, warm air is being sucked into a giant whirlpool up in the sky. As the air rises the pressure falls, in the area marked 'L'.

The concentric lines (isobars) around the low are lines of equal pressure: the closer these isobars, the windier the weather. Eventually, the cold front catches up with the warm front and lifts the warm air and the cool air ahead of it completely off the ground. This makes an occluded front (shown as a line with alternating semi-circles and triangles). You hardly notice the difference from the ground because the sky is usually covered in clouds, but it marks the dying throes of the depression. The low pressure in the middle begins to fill in, the winds abate and the clouds disperse.

This is an expanded view of diagram 5. It shows the line of contact of the warm front and the cold front above the ground.

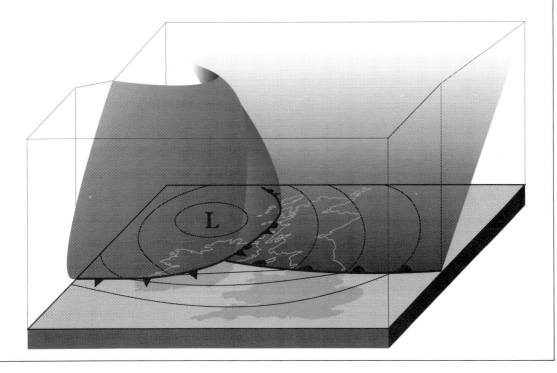

stratus) bringing heavy rain or snow, winds, and sometimes thunderstorms or even tornadoes. But the cold front passes quickly and afterwards the wind veers north-westerly, bringing clearer, brighter weather, and the clouds lift and thin to altostratus, cirrostratus and then cirrus, sometimes mixed with showers.

So there we have the typical warm and cold fronts you regularly see on weather maps. The fronts can vary in strength: if the depression is intense the weather on the fronts is more striking. On the other hand, a weak depression has fronts which do not bring much in the way of cloud and rain, and these are known as 'weak'.

The differences between warm and cold air masses are often not as dramatic as their weather systems suggest. There might only be one or two degrees in temperature difference between them.

OCCLUDED FRONTS: THE DYING DEPRESSION

Another common feature of weather maps is an occluded front. In the mature depression the cold front eventually catches up with the warm front and then lifts the cool air ahead of it, causing an occluded front, shown on weather maps as a purple line with alternating semi-circles and triangles. Seen from the ground an occlusion isn't much different from a cold front. The rain belt is narrow, and winds usually veer to the north or west behind it. There is usually a clearance from the west after the front has moved through.

At this stage the depression is very vigorous, with low pressure, strong winds and rain. But after the front becomes occluded the low starts to fill (pressure increases again) and the winds moderate and the depression becomes sluggish, often as it reaches Scandinavia. This is the death of the depression.

A typical depression lasts for about five days, but its character is changeable. Sometimes one depression is followed by another one. When the jet stream in the upper atmosphere becomes vigorous it often produces a family of depressions. Depending on their size and speed, they may come racing in at 24-hour intervals. If we are lucky the rain comes at night and the days bring reasonable weather between the depressions. Places that often get hit by depressions have very wet and windy weather. For instance, strong westerly winds from the sea slam straight into Shetland, the Hebrides and western Scotland. Once one depression has crossed Scotland, taking the gales towards Scandinavia, another approaches, often taking a slightly more southerly track towards western Ireland, Wales and Cornwall. But looking on the bright side, depressions tend to bring mild air in from the Atlantic during the winter. During the summer they bring rain and block out the sun. This may be irritating for holiday-makers, but often water companies are thankful for the rain.

ANTICYCLONES

As air descends in an anticyclone it dries out and warms up, and there is little or no upper cloud. If more air flows in from above than flows out at the surface the pressure increases, and the anticyclone becomes more intense. When an anticyclone arrives in Britain the weather tends to be fair and the winds light. We usually look on anticyclones or areas of high pressure as good news. They often bring dry weather but, because anticyclones tend to have clear skies, they can give very cold weather in the winter, letting heat escape from the earth, and so bring frost and sometimes fog. In summer they allow the sun to heat up the earth, bringing fine warm weather.

CONTINENTAL WEATHER

The typical bracing seaside breezes of a summer's day come from a simple bit of science. The sun heats up land faster than sea during the day so the air rises over the land and sinks over the sea. Meanwhile, the cool air from the sea flows in to take its place over the land: hence the bracing breeze. The opposite happens at night when the land cools down faster than the sea, and cooler air blows from the land over the sea.

On a much vaster scale, the same phenomenon explains why Continental weather is hot in the summer and cold in the winter. The sun heats up the land faster than the sea in summer, but in winter the land cools faster than the sea.

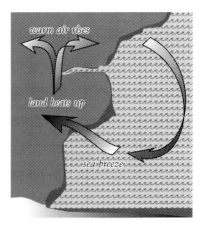

Those bracing seaside breezes of summer which keep kites airborne, yachts sailing and sunbathers cool are caused by cycles of air. During the day the land warms up strongly, and the warm air rises and blows out to sea where it cools and sinks. The cool air returns to land and heats up again, and so on. Sea breezes are strongest in the afternoon, but at night the breezes flow the other way, as the land cools down faster than the sea, so cooler air blows out to sea and the sea heats it up again. Land breezes are usually weaker than sea breezes.

45

The Weather Forecast

THE BRITISH WRITER Jerome K Jerome once remarked that no one would be happy until they had their own personal weather forecast. He had a point. Everyone, from farmers to fishermen, cab-drivers to commuters, listens to the daily weather forecast and makes plans accordingly. For some people the only decision is whether or not to take a raincoat to work tomorrow; for others, the forecast is vital in deciding whether to plant crops or put to sea.

The weather forecasters often receive complaints that the forecast was wrong. What the complainant usually means is that the forecast predicted 'sunny intervals and showers' for the South-East, and he or she was unlucky enough to get wet. Sometimes the reverse happens, for example when farmers desperate for rain ring up to complain that despite a forecast for 'some rain in East Anglia', the sky above their farm stayed obstinately dry.

These complaints, and the belief that the weathermen always get it wrong, are based on the simple fact that a forecast for the whole of the country, or even for a particular region, can only ever predict what will happen over a wide geographical area. It simply isn't possible to give everyone individually tailored forecasts for what will happen, weatherwise, over their heads! The weather just isn't that straightforward.

Despite the traditional British desire to blame the messenger, the daily weather forecasts issued by the Met. Office are remarkably accurate. The 24-hour forecast is now accurate 84 per cent of the time – that's five days out of every six – and the three-day forecast is now more accurate than the 24-hour forecast of two decades ago.

Of course, the Met. Office does sometimes get it wrong. Perhaps the most celebrated instance was on Thursday 15 October 1987, the day before the famous storm. During that evening's forecast, Michael Fish told viewers 'A woman has rung the BBC to say she's heard there's a hurricane on the way. Well, don't worry, there isn't!' As dawn broke the next day, south-east England was facing the worst storm devastation for more than two centuries. The subsequent row left the Met. Office with egg on their faces although, as they pointed out, the storm was so exceptional that no one could have foreseen its consequences. The row over the October 1987 storm brought the Met. Office into the public eye more than ever before. Ultimately this may prove to be beneficial, as more and more people realise the weather can't be taken for granted, and that forecasting what it will do is a very difficult job indeed.

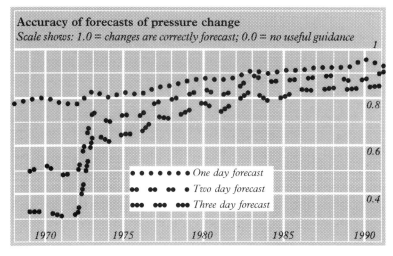

Accuracy of forecasts of pressure change
Scale shows: 1.0 = changes are correctly forecast; 0.0 = no useful guidance

- One day forecast
- Two day forecast
- Three day forecast

As most people have noticed, the weather forecast is getting more accurate. Today, the Met. Office's three-day forecast is actually more reliable than the 24-hour forecast of a couple of decades ago, but nobody can guarantee that a weather forecast will be 100 per cent accurate: it's beyond the capability of humans or computers.

THE HISTORY OF THE MET. OFFICE

Like the BBC, pubs and afternoon tea, the Met. Office is a British institution, yet its origins were humble. In 1854, a small department was formed at the Board of Trade to provide weather information for sailors. The first head of the department was Captain Robert FitzRoy, the master of the *Beagle* on Charles Darwin's famous voyage. Unfortunately for FitzRoy, the job of providing accurate predictions with minimal information proved impossible. When his forecasts were ridiculed, he killed himself by slitting his throat with a razor.

Since this unpromising start the Met. Office has gone from strength to strength. It first came to prominence during the First World War, when accurate forecasting was vital for military success. Between the wars, it was first suggested that more accurate forecasting could be gained with giant computers, but for many years the technology simply wasn't available to do such a complex job.

The first live television broadcasts came in 1954. The Met. Office moved in 1961 to its present headquarters in Bracknell, Berkshire. One year later the first electronic computer was installed, realising the dreams of the pioneering meteorologists. From then on, technology improved by leaps and bounds. Initially, in 1964, came the first satellite pictures of cloud formations; then, during the 1970s and 1980s, a succession of powerful computers was put into operation. They are essential for meteorologists, as they store the vast amount of data continually coming in from all over the world, and use it to make projections of what the weather is likely to do next.

In 1991, the Met. Office installed two Cray supercomputers. These are even faster and more complex than their predecessors, enabling the forecasts to be more up-to-date and more accurate than ever.

THE MET. OFFICE TODAY

Today, the Met. Office is the world's leading weather forecasting centre. We know it as the producer of our daily television and radio forecasts, but its work goes far beyond this. Responsible to the Secretary of State for Defence, it

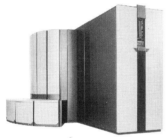

Above The Met. Office's Cray twins – two supercomputers which are among the most powerful in the world. They are used to analyse weather data from all round the world, and have helped to improve the accuracy of the weather forecast.

Facing page Forks of lightning make city lights pale into insignificance.

Left Waterspouts (the marine equivalent of tornadoes) are currently believed to be responsible for the weird showers of fishes, frogs and other creatures that occasionally rain down on unsuspecting people. The funnel of air is thought to suck up the creatures from the water and then release them, with their water, once the cloud passes inland.

Facing page This dramatic tornado, with its rapidly rotating funnel of air, was photographed in Texas in 1989.

Above High cirrus clouds, known as mare's tails, are wispy and composed of ice crystals. Weather folklore says that if the mare's tails point upwards, as these do, they indicate that rain is on the way.

Right These cumulonimbus clouds no longer threaten rain. The reduced heat from the setting sun has robbed them of their energy and they have started to decay.

Above Cumulus clouds
massing over the South
Downs. They can develop
from the small fluffy
clouds typical of a fine
summer's day into huge
storm-bringing
cumulonimbus clouds.

Left Altocumulus clouds
over Antarctica, with
patches of lenticular
altocumulus.

provides services in five major areas: to the Ministry of Defence (MOD) itself; to the Civil Aviation Authority; to industry and commerce; to the general public; and, finally, to the Department of the Environment's (DOE) climate research programme.

Each of these customers has special needs. The Met. Office's largest customer, the MOD, requires highly accurate local forecasts, especially for low-level flying, where advance warning of hazardous conditions can mean the difference between life and death.

Civil aviation, the biggest non-military customer, also requires detailed forecasts on weather conditions for take-off and landing, and *en route* at different levels of the atmosphere. The fishing and merchant fleets need the precise detail of the shipping forecast in order to avoid dangerous weather conditions. The offshore oil rigs can't move away from weather, so they need a pinpoint forecast of likely wave and wind conditions for up to eight days ahead. Severe weather conditions also affect the emergency services, so the Met. Office works closely with the police, fire and ambulance services to provide 'flash' messages, warning the public of expected problems.

Our major energy-providers, the electricity and gas industries, need to know what the weather will be because demand is dependent upon the weather, particularly the temperature. For the water industry, Met. Office information and advice is even more vital, especially during the present series of droughts. One of the commercial arms of the Met. Office, The Weather Initiative, provides forecasts and advice to a wide variety of industries and businesses in the retail sector (see Weather and our Wealth).

Given the recent worries about global warming, climate research is a vital part of the Met. Office's work. Since 1990, this has been carried out by the Hadley Centre for Climate Research, funded jointly by the DOE and the MOD. This research involves scientific investigation into the complicated behaviour of the atmosphere, and the creation of complex computer 'models', which help the researchers predict what may happen to the world's weather far into the future.

Above The Beaufort Scale is based on conditions at sea, and these photographs show a selection of wind speeds as experienced at sea. From the top, Force 4 (moderate breeze); Force 6 (strong breeze); Force 8 (gale); Force 10 (storm).

Facing page A fishing boat being tossed about on very stormy seas.

Right Anyone old enough to have watched television in 1954 may remember the BBC's George Cowling, who was the first television weather forecaster.

Facing page Nearly 40 years on, television weather forecasters have a much more relaxed and informal image. Ian McCaskill and John Kettley, shown here sporting some Met. Office merchandise, are household names, reflecting the British obsession with the weather.

The most familiar public faces of the Met. Office are those of the television and radio weather forecasters. People like Michael Fish, Bill Giles and Ian McCaskill are household names, as famous as soap opera stars and politicians, and rather more popular! These men (not to mention Bernard Davey, John Kettley, Rob McElwee, Peter Cockcroft and the one woman, Suzanne Charlton) are not only chosen for their skill at communicating with the public – they are also highly-skilled meteorologists, still employed as Civil Servants by the Met. Office.

Perhaps this explains their enduring popularity, despite attempts by rival television stations to glamorise the weather forecasts with 'weather girls', who often have little or no meteorological training. It seems that the viewing public wants the voice of authority that only a weather forecaster from the Met. Office can provide.

THE TELEVISION WEATHER FORECAST

Every day the familiar faces of the weather forecasters bring tomorrow's forecast direct to your homes, via your television set. But have you ever wondered how they know what to say? After all, they're stuck in a tiny room in the BBC Television Centre in West London – not the ideal place for knowing what the weather will be like in the rest of Britain!

The television weather forecast is a triumph of technology, human skills and the occasional flash of intuition. As you read this account it's worth remembering that the familiar forecasters, and their highly-skilled back-up team, provide television and radio forecasts around 50 times a day, every day of the year – including Christmas Day!

The key to accurate forecasting can be summed up in a single word: observation. Unless you know what the weather is doing now, you won't be able to predict what's going to happen in the future. However, you can't tell what the weather is doing just by looking out of the window! So the Met. Office has set up a huge network of observers to collect the raw data vital to successful forecasting. This is part of a worldwide observing network.

At the core of the operation are the hundred or so land-based stations scattered all over the country, from the Scilly Isles to Shetland. Some are in remote coastal spots, such as Tiree and Cape Wrath; others are at busy inland sites, such as Heathrow and Gatwick Airports. The most important ones take observations once an hour, day and night – every day of the year. There is also a network of around 2500 further observers filing reports once a day.

51

These land stations are backed up by a network of over 500 sea-based stations, including the Met. Office's own weather ship *Cumulus*, and the voluntary observing fleet, which all send regular observations back to the Met. Office headquarters in Bracknell. The Met. Office also runs a network of automatic stations, on land and sea, mostly situated in isolated places where human observers would find it impossible to live – such as on high mountains or over the continental shelf (the seaward extension of the land).

The familiar rainfall picture we see on television forecasts comes from weather radars. The ability to show movements of bands of rain can be incredibly useful, especially when an accurate prediction is required for a particular place and time, such as at a royal wedding or sporting event. An example of this occurred during Wimbledon fortnight in 1985. As a match neared its climax on Centre Court, the referee received a telephone call from Bill Giles. He warned there would be a sudden downpour within 15 minutes. Despite the clear skies, the referee took Bill's word, stopped play and covered the courts. Sure enough, 15 minutes later the heavens opened. The crowds got soaked, but the courts were saved! Soon, however, a further call confirmed the rain would stop within the next few minutes, and the rest of the day would be clear.

Other methods of collecting data are air-borne. Commercial airliners are fitted with automatic data-collectors, which report back every seven minutes. The Met. Office also release packages of instruments hanging below helium-filled balloons. As the balloons rise through the atmosphere to heights of more than 20 kilometres (12 miles), the instruments measure pressure, temperature and humidity, and radio back the data to the ground station. The position and movement of the balloon allows the wind speed and direction to be calculated. The information these balloons provide is essential for accurate forecasting, because it gives a vertical dimension to the weather above our heads. Last but not least, the meteorologists also use data from polar-orbiting and geostationary satellites, which send back the pictures of cloud patterns we see on the television forecasts.

From 'our man in Lerwick' to your front room

By following the course of a single weather report from the synoptic station at Lerwick, in the Shetland Isles, we can discover how the raw data and observations build up into the forecast you see on your television screen.

Lerwick is the most northerly 24-hour station in the British Isles, situated on the Shetland Isles at 60°08′ North, 1°11′ West. It's closer to Bergen in Norway than to Aberdeen, and as far north of Glasgow as Glasgow is north of London! The Lerwick observatory is 83 metres (272 feet) above sea level. It was built in 1922, and is staffed by 12 people, including four observers who work a daily shift pattern so the station can give 24-hour coverage. Here is the typical progress of one report from Lerwick, made at midday.

12.00 The duty observer makes the hourly observations and records data, such as temperature and rainfall. Beginning with the measurements, he reads:

● Atmospheric pressure using a precision aneroid barometer. This is converted to mean sea level pressure, so data taken at different altitudes are compatible. The change in pressure over the previous three hours is noted.

● Temperature either using a mercury/glass (the sort you might use at home) or electronic thermometer. This is housed in a wooden box, called a thermometer screen, to protect it from direct sunlight. The 'wet-bulb' temperature is also read from a thermometer covered in moist muslin, so the dew point, relative humidity and vapour pressure can be calculated.

● Maximum and minimum temperature readings, which indicate how high the temperature has risen and how low it has fallen since the previous reading, are taken twice a day by the observer.

● Wind speed and direction measured with an anemometer.

● Rainfall measured with a rain gauge six times a day. The rate of rainfall is also monitored.

Below The Campbell-Stokes recorder measures the hours of sunshine each day by focusing the sun's rays on to a special card. Modern weather stations now use an electronic device to measure solar energy.

Middle Temperature is measured using a thermometer, housed in a wooden box.

Bottom Wind speed is measured with an anemometer on a 10-metre (32–feet) high mast.

Other observations are more complex, so the observer must use his or her experience to make accurate estimates. These include:

● Total amount of cloud, cloud type and height.

● Visibility estimated from the furthest object the observer can see.

● What the weather is doing–for example, is it raining? If so, continuously or intermittently? And is it light, heavy or moderate? Are there any unusual conditions, such as a thunderstorm?

● What the weather has done in the past one, three and six hours – for example, has it rained or snowed?

● State of ground – is it dry, wet, frozen, snow-covered?

All this data is collected remarkably quickly and efficiently. It is then converted into codes consisting of long strings of five-figure numbers which are meaningless to most of us, but instantly readable by any trained meteorologist anywhere in the world.

12.08 Just eight minutes after collection, the coded data is sent on, by telex, to Bracknell, where the observation is checked for errors.

12.10–12.50 Selected data from all over the country are compiled into the hourly bulletin. This is sent to National Meteorological Services across Europe, and at midday and midnight, all over the world. At the same time, Bracknell receives return bulletins from all over Europe and the rest of the world.

By **12.10**, the new BBC Weather Centre in Shepherd's Bush (and all other United Kingdom stations) is receiving the information from that hour's data collection on their computer screens across the United Kingdom, via Bracknell.

12.35 By now, the Bracknell computer has plotted all available observations on the chart which covers the United Kingdom, and parts of the nearby Continent and the surrounding seas. This is sent by fax and a computer link to United Kingdom weather stations, including the BBC Weather Centre.

1240 onwards At this stage, the skill of the television forecaster comes into its own. He or she analyses the data, draws up the charts and takes a view on what is likely to happen to the weather, then selects and positions weather symbols, radar and satellite pictures and computer-generated forecasts of rain and so on, on a computer screen so they can be called up at the touch of a button. The forecaster doesn't have a written script, because the time allotted for the forecast can change at the very last minute!

One of the team of forecasters at the headquarters of the Met. Office at Bracknell, preparing a forecast using satellite pictures, charts, computers and human understanding.

Michael Fish in the BBC Weather Centre. The forecasters have to prepare and operate the television weather studio themselves in broadcasts that are transmitted live. There can be up to 43 television forecasts per day.

1257 The television forecaster presents the local area forecast for the afternoon and the following day, just before the news at one o'clock.

1327 The television forecaster presents the national forecast for the afternoon and the following day. He or she stands in the weather studio in front of a blue-lit screen on which the chart is very faintly projected. The picture you see at home shows the forecaster standing in front of the chart, but that is not the case and in fact it is added electronically between the camera and the transmitter.

Meanwhile, back at Bracknell . . .
From 1200 onwards Another team of forecasters in the Central Forecasting Office has been checking global data which the super-computer has queried. When this happens, or when there are gaps in the picture, they can add 'bogus' data to over-ride or support the observations that have been queried. This is the 'man-machine mix' which results in better analyses than either can manage alone.

1400 onwards The computer produces an analysis over Europe and the North Atlantic of the weather conditions as they were at 1200, and uses this and the laws of physics to produce a forecast for ten minutes into the future. Then using that as the analysis for 1210, it repeats the process to create a forecast for 1220, and so on, therefore building up to forecasts for up to two days ahead in ten-minute steps.

1425 The Chief Forecaster and his team confer about expected developments over the next 24 hours.

1500 Advice based on this discussion is telexed to the BBC Weather Centre and all other United Kingdom stations. An example might include:

> *This run of the model maintains the continued rapid development of Low 'C'. It will continue north-eastwards across the Highlands, and the winds ahead of the cold front may be a problem . . .*

1520 The computer runs a global analysis, followed by a forecast for up to six days ahead.

1535 The Chief Forecaster confers with the BBC and ITN forecasters and issues a more detailed forecast to all stations, for example:

> *Rain over Ireland and the SW associated with the warm front will move rapidly ENE to reach all areas by midnight . . .*

1545 The medium-range forecaster starts to look at the output from the global model. He completes the forecasts for two to five days ahead for the North Atlantic and Europe. After discussion with the Chief Forecaster the information is sent by fax to all United Kingdom stations, where they are used for client services such as tʰ ` five-day farmers' forecast.

By now you can see what a complex operation it is to tell you whether or not to take an umbrella to work tomorrow!

Weather Lore and Traditional Forecasting

L ONG BEFORE THE DAYS of the official weather forecast, country people had to rely on their instincts and experience to predict the weather. Accuracy was crucial: in an age when most people lived off the land, a reliable forecast could mean the difference between prosperity and starvation.

Later in this chapter we will meet the diminishing band of forecasters who still rely on ancient techniques to predict the weather. But first, let's take a look at weather lore – the vast number of proverbs, sayings and old wives' tales about the weather that are still in use today. Is weather lore just a ragbag collection of quaint rhymes, or does it contain a grain of truth that might help us to predict the unpredictable?

WEATHER LORE

There have been sayings about the weather since the beginning of recorded time. Perhaps the best-known, 'Red sky at night, Shepherd's delight . . .', is even mentioned in the New Testament book of Matthew: 'When it is evening, ye say, it will be fair weather, for the sky is red.'

In most cases, the origin of these sayings is unknown, but it seems likely that most began as simple observations by country folk which held true for a particular place or season, and so were turned into rhymes or proverbs to make them easier to remember.

Despite the huge advances in high-tech weather forecasting, these sayings are as popular as ever. One researcher, Paul John

The king of the traditional folklore forecasters – Yorkshireman William Foggitt. He bases his forecasts on how the weather affects birds, plants and animals in the countryside around his home. But can he beat the Met. Office?

Goldsack, found almost 3000 weather proverbs in Britain alone. So why have they survived so long? Nostalgia apart, it's probably because some sayings hold at least a grain of truth, and a few actually do have a real value as accurate predictors of coming weather.

The list of weather sayings on the facing page shows which ones are the most accurate, as well as those likely to result in a nasty shock for anyone who relies on them! The ones that fail try to predict the weather in the coming season from a single event – an exercise doomed to failure. Try reversing them, and you might have better luck!

THE STORIES BEHIND THE PROVERBS

As we can see from the Top Ten table, sayings that predict the coming weather from the condition of the sky at the time are usually the most accurate. Incidentally, some of our most famous weather sayings just miss their place in the Top Ten by a whisker, scoring 69 per cent. These include 'Rain before seven, fine before eleven' and 'Red sky at night, shepherd's delight; red sky in the morning, shepherd's warning'. The reason 'Red sky at night . . .' is near the top of the weather sayings league is that it is, by and large, true. When clouds are tinged red by the setting sun, this means drier air to the west. In Britain, the prevailing winds come from the west or south-west, so a soft red sky indicates dry weather approaching. But take care! If the sky is an angry, dark red colour, the very opposite is the case – the next day will be wet and stormy! This can occur at any time of day, but is most common in the hours after dawn, hence the second part of the rhyme, 'Red sky in the morning, shepherd's warning'.

It's not just red skies that foretell the weather. Any strong, unusual colour usually means bad weather. Grey skies can mean good or bad weather. The saying 'Evening red and morning grey, two good signs for one fine day . . .' refers to the grey of morning mist, which often indicates a fine day once the sun has broken through. However, an approaching depression is also marked by grey skies. As with most weather lore, the observer's experience is vital.

WEATHER SAYINGS AND PROVERBS

Top Ten

Many sayings scored right more than two out of three times. Here are the most reliable (with their percentage of accuracy in brackets):

1 'Hoar-frost and gypsies never stay nine days in a place' (99%).

2= 'If there is a profuse dew in summer, it is about seven to one that the weather will be fine' (88%).

2= 'A white frost never lasts more than three days' (88%).

4 'If rain begins at early morning light, 'twill end ere day at noon is bright' (87%).

5 'March buys winter's cloak and sells it three days afterwards' (i.e. a spell of cold weather in March rarely lasts more than three days) (78%).

6 'The farther the sight, the nearer the rain' (i.e. good visibility means rain to follow within 24 hours) (77%).

7 'If cold on St Peter's Day [22 February] it will last longer' (i.e. longer than normal) (75%).

8 'The south wind, during the winter months, will bring mild, cloudy weather, with drizzle' (73%).

9 'The greater the haze the more settled the weather' (i.e. dry weather for at least three following days) (71%).

10 'When the wind's in the south, the rain's in its mouth' (i.e. it will rain within 24 hours) (70%).

Bottom Ten

No less than 15 sayings scored a duck – being right absolutely no times at all! These include (with the number of times they were tested in brackets):

1 'The weather that comes in with the moon stays like it for a month' (161).

2 'There are a hundred days of easterly wind in the first half of the year' (111).

3 'If the 18 last days of February be wet, and the first 10 of March, you'll see, that the spring quarter and the summer too, will prove too wet' (111).

4 'The night of St Peter [22 February] shows what weather we shall have for the next forty days' (106).

5 'Where the wind is at twelve o'clock on 21 March, there she'll bide for three months afterwards' (106).

6 'Where the wind is on Martinmas Eve [10 November], there it will be throughout the coming winter' (106).

7 'Wherever the wind lies on Ash Wednesday, it continues during all Lent' (94).

8 'If it rains on 27 June, it will rain seven weeks' (45).

9 'If October and November be snow and a frost, then January and February are like to be open and mild' (44).

10 'If it freezes on St Matthias's Day [24 February], it will freeze for a month together' (43).

Compiled from research by Paul J Marriott. For more details, see Marriott's book *Red Sky at Night, Shepherd's Delight*.

Cows sitting down – is rain imminent?

Rooks – reliable weather forecasters?

'Rain before seven, fine before eleven . . .' is another good predictor of the day to come. Again, this relies on what is a typical weather pattern in the British Isles: a depression bringing a belt of rain across the country. In most cases the rain will have passed over in three or four hours. However, the saying is only accurate about two-thirds of the time, so take an umbrella just in case!

Clouds and their patterns give rise to many sayings, the most well-known being the belief that a mackerel sky (high clouds creating a stippled effect) foretells unsettled, showery weather. Other theories are more complex: for instance, if cirrus clouds (or mare's tails) have their tails pointing upward, there will be rain; if downward, then fine weather is due. There is also a wide range of sayings suggesting that good visibility means bad weather to come, such as the Cornish saying 'When the Lizard is clear, rain is near'. This is because good visibility indicates a polar airstream, which generally brings showers.

Proverbs based on observing wild and domestic animals, birds and plants are far less reliable. Indeed, some well-known ones are so inaccurate that it's hard to see how they have lasted so long. Proverbially, cows are supposed to lie down before the approach of rain. They may well do so, but as they also lie down at many other times they are hardly reliable forecasters! Cows do sometimes react to changes in the weather: in common with most animals, including pet dogs, they may become agitated if a thunderstorm approaches. The problem with animals is that there may be all kinds of explanations for their unusual behaviour, so weather predictions based on this alone will often be wrong.

Nevertheless, there are some reliable proverbs based on animals and birds. High-flying swallows or swifts are usually an indication of good weather the following day, because they are feeding on insects which stay close to cover when rain is due. Rooks, too, are fairly reliable: in many parts of the country it's said that if rooks fly straight from their nests, the weather that day will be fine, but if they twist and turn, 'tumbling' in the air, rain will follow.

Like the ones based on the condition of the sky, many of these sayings are highly local in origin. Furthermore, what holds true for one part of the country may not work elsewhere, even a few miles away, where the weather patterns are different. So take the sayings with a pinch of salt!

You might need a barrelful of salt for another group of weather proverbs! Predictions of weather for the coming season, based on the weather on one particular day, are among the most common sayings. Yet a study of their accuracy, by amateur meteorologist P J Goldsack, found that not one long-term prediction was reliable, and most were highly misleading.

The continuing fame of an obscure ninth-century bishop named Swithin is entirely due to medieval superstition. A modest sort of chap, Swithin decreed that he should be buried outdoors when he died, in a place where the rain would fall on him. More than a century after his death, on 15 July 972, an attempt was made to rebury his body in Winchester Cathedral. It is said that his spirit was so outraged that rain fell for 40 days and nights afterwards, hence the verse:

> *St Swithin's Day if it do rain,*
> *for 40 days it will remain.*
> *St Swithin's Day if it be fair,*
> *for 40 days will rain no more.*

Forty days of continuously settled or unsettled weather is almost unknown in the British Isles, although the long hot summer of 1976 is a notable exception. However, Swithin can be well wide of the mark, too, as in 1924, when unbroken sunshine on 15 July was followed by almost continuous rain for the next month! The only grain of truth in the verse is that our summer weather tends to follow set patterns: it is either settled, sunny weather governed by dominant high pressure, or a series of depressions bringing rain and showers.

St Swithin's Day is only the best-known of a whole series of seasonal sayings. Virtually every saint's day is supposed to foretell the entire weather pattern for the coming season. On Candlemas (2 February), the depth of the sunshine coming through the window is supposed to predict the depth of

St Swithin – the first forecaster?

coming snow; on St Martin's Day (11 November), the weather is said to predict the severity of the coming winter. But whatever the prediction, sayings claiming to forecast the weather for the coming season have one thing in common – they are spectacularly inaccurate.

Perhaps we shouldn't be surprised – after all, if the Met. Office with all its powerful computers and accumulated expertise shies away from long-term seasonal forecasts, then we would hardly expect long-dead saints to have the power of the crystal ball. Two things are odd: that these sayings started up in the first place, and that they've lasted so long, instead of being consigned to the dustbin of oblivion.

Perhaps the only explanation for their continued popularity is that these ancient country sayings fulfil a vital human need. In our high-tech, modern world, in which we're further removed from the experiences of our ancestors than ever before, they provide a tangible link with our rustic roots.

TRADITIONAL FORECASTING

Weather proverbs, together with a whole range of superstitions, folklore and a lifetime's experience, are still employed by a band of traditional forecasters.

The undoubted king of the 'seaweed and frogspawn' brigade is Yorkshireman William Foggitt. Now in his late seventies, Bill Foggitt relies on a vast knowledge of local conditions around his native Thirsk to confound the Met. Office. His fame has spread in recent years, as the popular press seizes on any evidence, however flimsy, to try to prove the official forecasters wrong!

Bill's forecasts are based largely on the behaviour and movements of birds, animals and plants around his home. For example, in January 1989 he predicted a 'Freezing Febrrr-uary'. Fieldfares were migrating south, hedgehogs were beginning to hibernate and Bill was awaiting the arrival of a woodpecker in his garden – a sure sign of a cold spell to come, he said. However, the Met. Office Monthly Weather Report for February 1989 shows he got it wrong, stating 'it was a very mild month in most places'. At Leeming, North Yorkshire,

Above A stunning sunset over Horsey Mere in Norfolk.

Left This winter sunrise in Lincolnshire is a fine example of cirrocumulus clouds, commonly known as a mackerel sky.

Facing page
Cumulonimbus clouds gathering over the South Pacific.

Right A pale mackerel sky (altocumulus) in Iceland.

Following pages
Altocumulus floccus clouds with altocumulus lenticularis, looking like a flying tortoise, in the foreground.

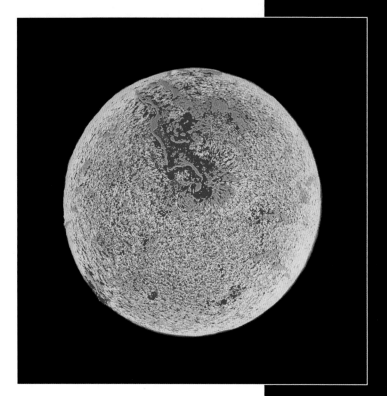

Above A false-colour image of the sun, showing sunspots (green dots), active regions (large red areas) and filaments (green lines). Sunspots, which often occur in groups, are pockets of relatively cool dark gas in magnetically active regions. A filament is a jet of hot gas shooting up into the sun's corona.

Right The aurora borealis, also known as the northern lights, are seen in the night sky at high latitudes and are often red or green in colour. Auroras are caused by charged particles from the sun colliding with atoms of oxygen and nitrogen in the atmosphere.

the nearest weather station to Thirsk, the mean temperature was a mild 5.9°C (42.6°F), and there were only four days of frost all month.

Undaunted, in May of the same year, Bill was at it again. He'd noticed the frogs laying their spawn in the centre of his garden pond, rather than at the edges. This, he suggested, meant we were in for a spell of hot, dry weather. Bees were abundant, too, calling to mind the proverb 'Bees in May mean a load of hay'; and swallows and cuckoos had arrived earlier than usual. This time, Bill's prediction was spot on – the summer of 1989 was one of the hottest since records began.

Can the predictions made by Bill Foggitt and his fellow country forecasters really foretell long-term changes in the weather? The Met. Office is sceptical. They point out that any observed reactions of animals or plants are almost certainly due to existing conditions, so can only be used for very short-term predictions. Also, the causes of these reactions may vary. For example, just because seaweed goes damp doesn't necessarily mean wet weather is to come. Seaweed does absorb moisture when the air is getting damper as rain approaches, but it also does so when dew is forming during a fine night, which would indicate good weather the following day!

Amateur forecasting isn't confined to men of the country-side. Until he died in the autumn of 1990, retired bank clerk Arthur Mackins was one of Britain's most successful amateur forecasters. Living in retirement in Bognor, he scorned both 'folklore and fancy computers' as a means of forecasting the weather. Instead, he relied on the study of long-term historical records, and his own trusty barometer.

He worked out a complex series of weather cycles which he used to make long-term forecasts. These included no fewer than three separate cycles for hot, dry summers: a seven-year cycle (for example, the summers of 1969, 1976, 1983 and 1990); a fourteen-year cycle (1975 and 1989); and even a ten-year cycle based on years ending in 9. With this variety of possibilities it's perhaps surprising that poor summers could get a look-in, but Arthur had a cycle for these too – years ending in the number 8.

Facing page A large volcanic eruption, such as this one at Mount St Helens in America, can have long-term meteorological consequences that may be just as harmful as man-made pollution.

Arthur Mackins claimed a 90 per cent success rate, and certainly had some spectacular successes. He came to national notice in 1971, when he countered the Met. Office's prediction of a wet July with the view that the month would turn out to be 'a scorcher'. He was right. Then in the mid-1970s he successfully predicted the two drought summers of 1975 and 1976, but let himself down by going for the hat-trick in 1977. This time, he was wrong. His run of bad luck continued when in 1980 he predicted good summer weather in no less a reliable organ than *The Times* newspaper. When the summer turned out to be a disappointment, Arthur swiftly placed the blame on the eruption of the Mount St Helens volcano, thousands of miles away in Washington state. *The Times* gratefully seized on this excuse.

Arthur was to have the last laugh, however. In the spring of 1990 he predicted that the previous very mild winter meant a very hot summer. Summer 1990 broke all records, including the highest ever recorded temperature in the United Kingdom, topping 37°C (98.8°F) in Cheltenham. After that triumph, Arthur Mackins packed up his barometer and record books, and went to that great weather station in the sky.

In doing so, he missed perhaps the greatest collective mistake of the amateur forecasters, the non-existent white Christmas of 1990. This time, the traditional forecasters and the retired Met. men, the high-tech consultants and the country sages were all in agreement. Bookmakers were snowed under with bets at generous odds of around 10 to 1.

It all began on St Martin's Day, 11 November, traditionally the day which foretells the weather of the winter to come. Bill Foggitt had seen some Bewick's swans from Siberia arriving much earlier than usual, and the weather had been unusually mild, bringing to mind the proverb 'If ducks swim at Hallowtide, at Christmas the ducks will slide'. In East Anglia, squirrels had been 'weighed down with walnuts'; in Scotland, a retired Met. Office man had seen geese flying high, 'a sure sign that winter will come early'. Even the high-tech experts agreed. Piers Corbyn of the consultancy Weatherplan Services had placed a bet of £100 with bookmakers William Hill. If there was a white Christmas, he stood to gain £1000.

November 1990 was generally dry and sunny, especially in the south and west. December was changeable, with a cold spell during the second week. From 20 December, a succession of fast-moving fronts crossed the United Kingdom, bringing strong winds and bands of rain, and even sleet and snow in the north.

On Christmas Eve, bookmakers all over Britain prepared to spend what might prove to be, if the amateur forecasters were right, their final prosperous Christmas before being plunged into penury. Punters rubbed their hands with glee at the anticipation of a Christmas windfall. The Met. Office declined to make any firm prediction until a day or two before, reasoning that the degree of accuracy required was impossible to achieve so far ahead.

Meanwhile, at the London Weather Centre, 19-year-old observer Angus Stronach prepared himself for a lonely vigil. It had fallen to him to be one of the two arbiters of whether Christmas 1990 would be white. He had volunteered to spend two consecutive 12-hour night shifts at the Weather Centre, watching and waiting for a snowflake to fall on the roof. Incidentally, the definition of a white Christmas, as far as the bookmakers are concerned, is that a flake of snow must fall on the roof of the London Weather Centre between the hours of midnight on Christmas Eve and midnight on Christmas Day – snow already lying there doesn't count!

Angus' lonely vigil was in vain. The amateurs had got it wrong, the Met. Office was right, and once again Britain's long run of grey Christmases continued. In fact, the highest temperature of the month was recorded in nearby Greenwich on Boxing Day – an unseasonally mild 14.6°C (58°F).

A glance at the record books shows just how gullible the punters were. There have only been four true white Christmases in Central London this century: in 1906, 1927, 1938 and the most recent in 1970. In 1981 there was deep snow on the ground on Christmas Day, but none fell on the actual day itself. So that year, at least, both the bookmakers and the children were happy!

Weather and the Natural World

O F ALL LIVING CREATURES, birds are the ones most affected by changes in the weather. The reason is simple: they spend a large proportion of their lives in the air, whether feeding, courting or migrating, and so are uniquely vulnerable to the weather's influence.

WEATHER AND BIRDS

For some birds, the very ability to fly is at the mercy of the weather. Large, heavy birds, such as eagles, vultures and buzzards, require a huge expenditure of energy to get airborne – energy which they may not be able to replace easily, so they rely on thermals (rising currents of warm air) on which they soar on their broad wings. Within a remarkably short time an eagle can rise almost out of sight on a thermal.

All birds, large or small, are dependent on the weather for one aspect of their lifecycle – breeding. Like us, when spring is in the air, birds' thoughts turn to courtship! However, birds can be fooled by unseasonally mild weather. During November and December 1953 the weather in Britain was unusually mild – more than 5°C (9°F) above normal. Birds like the blackbird and song thrush took this as a cue for nest-building, and some even managed to raise their young before the true winter weather arrived. Even spring weather can cause problems, such as when birds lay their eggs in mild weather, only to be caught out by the onset of frost or snow which can make the eggs infertile.

Migration is another aspect of bird behaviour governed by the weather. The mechanics of how birds navigate is still shrouded in mystery, but we know the sun and stars play an important part. To begin migration, birds require fairly clear skies. Yet despite their sensitivity to changes in weather conditions they can still get caught out. Occasionally robins, thrushes and warblers will set off southwards from Scandinavia in good weather, but get caught by rain and wind *en route*. When this happens, they will seek shelter on the nearest land or, if there's none available, on oil-rigs and lighthouses! At its most spectacular, this phenomenon causes 'falls' of migrants on the British east coast. After one spectacular fall in September 1965, more than 12 000 robins were counted on one short stretch of beach in Kent.

Birds and weather folklore

As noted in the last chapter, many country sayings and old wives' tales are based on the observation of birds' behaviour. The best-known ones are said to predict a change for the worse: heavy rain or storms. Some local names of birds refer to this. The missel thrush is known to this day in rural areas as the storm cock, because of its habit of singing as a storm approaches. The green woodpecker has been christened the rain bird, or in Somerset the wet bird, because of the belief that its laughing call heralds the coming of rain. And in Scotland, the red-throated diver is sometimes known as the rain goose, again because its eerie, haunting call is said to mean rain. As the bird breeds mainly in Shetland, Orkney and north-west Scotland, which are some of the wettest parts of Britain, this may be just coincidence! Because of its habit of hovering motionless in the wind, the kestrel has acquired a variety of local weather names, including windhover (made famous by the poet Gerard Manley Hopkins).

Several official bird names refer to the weather. The name of the storm petrel appears to have originated with sailors, who associated the appearance of this ocean-going bird with the coming of bad weather. The snow bunting, a winter visitor to our shores, is known in parts of Scotland as the snow flake.

The kestrel was given its alternative name of windhover because of its ability to hover motionless in the wind.

The missel thrush is often known as the storm cock because of its habit of singing before a storm.

69

Small birds often need food and water if they are to survive harsh winters.

Recent cold winters almost destroyed the rare Dartford warbler.

Birds and extreme weather

Birds are very vulnerable to harsh weather, either because of loss of food supplies covered by snow or ice, or simply because heat loss can lead to death. Smaller birds usually roost together at night, and some species, notably the starling, take advantage of the fact that our urban areas are warmer at night than the surrounding countryside. Each winter evening, just before sunset, many city centres are filled with the calling of tens of thousands of starlings going to roost, the best-known being in London's Leicester Square.

During the winter, an impending snowstorm will often be preceded by vast movements of birds flying south and west, away from the coming bad weather. Some may even move on to the Continent, leaving parts of eastern Britain almost devoid of common birds like blue and great tits. If you notice a steady stream of birds in the skies heading south or south-west in winter, the chances are high that bad weather will follow within 24 hours. Conversely, if there is bad weather on the Continent, wintering ducks and grebes will move westwards from the Netherlands to the reservoirs and gravel-pits of south-east England, as happened in the winter of 1978–9.

Some species find it impossible to move far, because of their specialised habitat and feeding requirements. The consecutive cold winters of 1961–2 and 1962–3 virtually wiped out the population of the rare heathland species the Dartford warbler. The same happened in 1978, when a hard spell in February more than halved the population of 400 pairs. Fortunately, a succession of mild winters since has enabled the species to recolonise many of its former haunts in southern England.

Water feeders like the heron and water rail are hard-hit by freezing weather too, as they cannot get to their food. In harsh winters, normally shy species such as the kingfisher and bittern are often reported in parks and towns, and even seen trying to feed from iced-over garden ponds. Small birds, too, are vulnerable to hard winters: the wren, Britain's commonest bird, suffered a decline of nearly four-fifths of its population during the severe winter of 1962–3. One way to reduce the death toll is to put out food and water – vital for birds whose usual sources of water for drinking and bathing are frozen. The Royal Society for the Protection of Birds believes that food put out on bird-tables makes a very real contribution to the survival of familiar garden birds such as the blue tit and robin.

Long-term climatic change also affects Britain's bird population. The red-backed shrike, or butcher bird, was a familiar sight in country lanes as recently as the Second World War. However, a gradual change to wetter, more unsettled summers, has reduced the population of beetles and dragonflies essential to the shrike's diet. One pair hung on in the East Anglian Brecks until the late 1980s, but the bird is now extinct as a British breeding species.

During cold winter nights starlings keep warm by roosting together on the tops of buildings.

Weather and global wanderers

Perhaps the most interesting way in which the weather affects our birds is seen each spring and autumn, as wandering vagrants from as far afield as South-East Asia, Africa and North America arrive exhausted on our shores. Some of these birds, each one little bigger than a blue tit and weighing a fraction of an ounce, have been driven more than 16 000 kilometres (10 000 miles) off-course by freak weather conditions and cause excitement to birdwatchers.

In spring, these birds tend to be overshooting migrants, returning from Africa to their breeding grounds in southern Europe. If high pressure is dominant over the Mediterranean, such exotic beauties as bee-eaters, hoopoes and egrets may turn up, most frequently at south coast sites such as Beachy Head, Dungeness or Portland Bill.

In autumn, unusual birds come from the east, brought thousands of miles overland by strange weather condi-

tions; and from the west, driven across the Atlantic in the prevailing south-westerly airstream. These birds, mainly American wood-warblers, cuckoos and thrushes, have to cross thousands of miles of ocean to reach any landfall, so it's a miracle any survive at all. That some do is largely due to the speed of the winds which bring them here. Most are displaced as they migrate southwards on their way to spend the winter in the Caribbean or South America. Taking the shortest route along the east coast of Canada and the United States, they fly out to sea. When this coincides with the onset of a strong, south-westerly airstream, they are blown off-course and out into the Atlantic. The vast majority perish, but a lucky few are swept along by the windstream, crossing the ocean in as little as two or three days. Living on stored fat resources, and occasionally taking shelter on passing ships, these tiny birds arrive exhausted on the south-west coasts of Britain and Ireland, to delight thousands of 'twitchers' – birdwatchers whose main aim is to see rare birds.

But where do these avian wanderers go? Many die, exhausted and starving, soon after landing in Europe. Others try to re-orientate themselves and either perish in the Atlantic, or turn up unexpectedly further south. One thing is sure: because of the prevailing south-westerly direction of the winds, none will ever sing again in the woods and prairies of North America.

A wind-blown storm petrel takes a rest on a passing ship.

WEATHER AND PLANTS

The proverbial bit of seaweed is supposed to be a good forecaster of rain, but flowers are probably a lot more sensitive, and many of them probably grow in your garden as weeds or garden plants. If the scarlet pimpernel (also known as the poor man's weather glass) closes its flowers in the daytime it signals rain, and if they open they tell of fair weather. There are many other weather forecasting plants that close their flowers at the approach of rain, including the Siberian sow-thistle, *Sonchus siberius*; the African marigold, *Tagetes erectus*; the bindweed *Convolvulus arvensis*; the marigold, *Calendula pluvialis*; the goat's beard, *Clematis*; the dandelion, *Tarax-*

acum; and the ox-eye daisy, *Chrysanthemum vulgare*.

There's some scientific basis to these predictions. Flowers are desperate to avoid getting their pollen wet, which might otherwise sprout prematurely, so they have developed a keen sense of moisture which forecasts wet weather: for instance, the scarlet pimpernel closes its petals when the relative humidity reaches 80 per cent. When the humidity drops the flowers re-open, which is why hay fever is always worst on fine dry days, when flowers (particularly grasses) are showering their pollen into the air. The trouble with relying on weather prediction from flowers is that they also close at night-time and have their own natural closing rhythms. They also respond to mist or damp fog in otherwise settled weather.

Many flowers tell of wet weather. The ox-eye daisy (*left*), scarlet pimpernel (*above*) and many others close their flowers or flower heads in damp air, helping to protect their pollen from sprouting prematurely.

Plants are very sensitive to the wind. They respond to it by strengthening their stems, trunks and branches to prevent themselves being blown over. This windswept tree has taken matters to extremes by putting all its growth on to one side to withstand constant buffeting.

Leaves

The most famous leafy forecaster is *Abrus precatorius*, a member of the bean family that grows wild in India. On any normal day it can be seen raising and lowering its branches and folding and unfolding its leaves. If you touch a leaf the entire branch will fold up. The plant also folds up at night or when rain or hail touches its leaves. The plant became known as the 'weather plant' in 1887, when Joseph Nowak applied for an English patent to use it as a weather forecaster. Even though his patent application failed he claimed that if young

leaves from the north side of a plant showed unusual movements then thunderstorms were supposed to arrive from that
direction in two days' time. If the leaf stalk moved the
branches vigorously up and down then an earthquake was
predicted!

The trouble with all these leaf movements is that the plants
are sensitive to their own internal rhythms, the quality of
daylight and temperature, and they all close at dusk, so cannot
be relied upon to forecast the weather.

HOW PLANTS ARE AFFECTED BY WEATHER
The weather affects plants in many ways, some of which they
adapt to quite naturally.

Wind
You'd hardly think wind makes much of a difference to plants
one way or the other, but under windy weather (and that
means breezes as well as gales) they grow thicker and more
stunted stems – a sensible way of steeling themselves against
the ravages of the wind. In fact, trees even grow a special sort
of wood, called reaction wood, on the leeward side of the wind
to strengthen their trunks and branches. Just look at the
windswept trees on top of cliffs. They're convincing testimony
to the sensitivity of plants to wind.

Drought
The fearsome drought suffered by southern England during
these past few summers has tested our plant life to the limit. At
the first signs of drought plants trigger off alarm signals, telling
their leaf pores (stomata) to close to prevent wilting and
slowing down growth in readiness for tough times ahead.

Leaf movements are a common solution to drought in wild
plants. The marram grasses growing on sand dunes can have
an exceptionally dry life, which they cope with by rolling their
slender leaves into tubes to protect their stomata from the
drying effect of wind. The so-called tropical air-plants, which
grow over telephone wires and anywhere else they can get a
toetold, have moisture-sensitive plugs attached to their leaf

pores. When the weather gets too dry the stalks contract so the plugs are pulled down to seal over the stomata. In wet weather, when it's safe to re-open the pores, the plugs do so.

Desert plants have the most ingenious ways of coping with drought. The lupin *Lupinus arizonicus* tracks the sun through the day with its mobile leaves but, towards noon, the leaves swivel away side-on to avoid the scorching midday sun. Cacti have simply dispensed with leaves and photosynthesise (use light to convert water and carbon dioxide into carbohydrates) with their fat stems. They also stay succulent and juicy by pumping themselves full of water using a concentrated sap of salts, sugars and amino acids. Under severe drought plants like the resurrection plant shrivel up into a dehydrated state of suspended animation, but at the first taste of water they reflate into their proud former selves and carry on life as normal.

Leaves and rainfall or warmth
Leaves can be very sensitive to rain, and with good reason. In the dark, dank understories of a tropical rainforest, leaves have to fight for every speck of daylight that filters through. If a film of rainwater builds up on the leaf surface it prevents the daylight reaching the leaf and starves it of photosynthesis. The leaves of the tropical liana, *Machaerium arboreum*, and even our wood sorrel, *Oxalis acetosella*, have slightly touch-sensitive leaves. They sense the pounding of a heavy rainfall and gracefully fold their leaves down to drain off the water.

Not all leaves move because they're wet. A lot of leaves fold down at night as if they're going to sleep. It took the courage of Charles Darwin to claim this was an adaptation to climate, so as to keep temperate and tropical mountain plants warm at night. For over a hundred years Darwin has been ridiculed for his suggestion, but recent evidence bears him out. When plants fold their leaves down they keep their tender buds and young leaves warm by a degree or two – enough to protect them against a chilly night. This is especially important for plants such as *Espeletia*, which grows in the Andes. This giant artichoke-like specimen literally rolls its leaves up into a ball at night and re-opens them at dawn to catch the morning light.

Waterlogging

Heavy and prolonged showers of rain can spell disaster for most plants. They become waterlogged and their roots are starved of the oxygen they need to survive. At the first signs of waterlogging the leaf pores are closed to prevent water flooding in through them and drowning the leaves. Then the plant suddenly puts on a spurt of growth, stretching upwards – hopefully to rise above the flood waters into fresh air.

Yet some plants positively thrive on waterlogging. Rice plants have to grow in waterlogged fields; the leaves of the plant are sculptured into tiny ridges which trap a film of air, and act as snorkels through which the stomata breathe.

Freezing weather

Freezing weather causes the same problems for plants as for household plumbing – once water freezes it expands and when it melts it contracts. That expansion and contraction bursts plant cells just like metal pipes, so the hardy plants have invented an ingenious range of strategies for bypassing the frost damage. Their most obvious way is by lagging themselves with insulation, like the bark on trees. They also often employ antifreezes like sugars, salts and even the same glycol antifreeze used in car radiators, which keeps their freezing point below 0°C (32°F) and stops ice crystallising.

Many plants have developed another knack for coping with temperatures below −40°C (−40°F) without freezing, using a phenomenon called supercooling. Put simply, freezing water has to make ice crystals around specks of some impurity – dust, dirt or anything else. The supercooled plant keeps its plumbing so scrupulously clean of foreign bodies that the ice crystals are left out in the cold, so to speak.

Perhaps the most bizarre cold-resistant plant is the rhododendron: the buds of the plant literally freeze-dry themselves before winter. As soon as it gets cold, the sap inside the delicate buds is syphoned out, leaving behind dehydrated tissues which can survive below −30°C (−22°F). The following spring the buds rehydrate and the buds burst open, giving the rhododendron a flying start to the new season.

Weather and our Health

WE'VE ALWAYS KNOWN that the weather affects our health: we feel good when the sun shines, and miserable when it rains. When someone is ill, we say they're 'under the weather'. Winter colds and 'flu, and summer sunburn and hay fever, are annual reminders of the effect the weather has on our bodies.

The seventeenth-century poet John Taylor summed up our sensitivity to the weather:

> *Some men by painful elbow, hip or knee*
> *Will shrewdly guess what weather's like to be . . .*

Even today, people claim that their aches and pains get worse or better with changes in the weather.

The belief that the weather influences our health isn't just ancient superstition. The weather is one of the biggest causes of rises in the death rate, and we are only just beginning to discover its long-term effect on our bodies. Current research by a new breed of scientists, called biometeorologists, suggests that, in the future, the weather will play an even greater role in determining our health.

BIOMETEOROLOGY

Biometeorology, and its sister science bioclimatology, are the studies of the respective influences of the weather and climate on our living selves. Our reactions to the weather depend on a variety of factors – our age, sex, general state of health, what we eat and where we live. However, they all have one thing in common – they are governed by our endocrine system, the system of glands which regulates the production of hormones in our bodies. Changes in the weather can have as profound an effect on the endocrine system as other influences like stress and pain.

Biometeorologists have estimated that, worldwide, around one in three people react to changing weather conditions. Not everyone is equally sensitive, of course, and vulnerable groups such as the elderly, infants and the chronically ill are much more likely to suffer. Women are especially sensitive, making up three-quarters of the affected population. It's thought that this is because women's bodies secrete fewer male hormones, making them more sensitive to changing conditions.

PHYSICAL REACTIONS TO THE WEATHER

Extreme conditions, such as heatwaves and sudden cold spells, affect us most strongly. Hot weather brings an increase in minor skin complaints, fainting and sunstroke, which are all caused by the body's reaction to increased heat. The heart rate goes up, blood vessels dilate to allow more blood to reach the skin's surface (for cooling purposes) and we sweat more. The combination of dehydration and loss of blood from the central nervous system can lead to collapse. In most cases the condition can be cured by such simple but effective remedies as lying somewhere cool, drinking plenty of liquid and replacing lost salt.

For one group of people, however, a heatwave can spell death. Elderly people are far less able to cope with sudden changes in the weather. Because their bodies are less efficient at reacting to the heat, a pressure-cooker effect can result, greatly increasing the chances of death. During the July 1983 heatwave, the number of deaths rose by over 1500 per week, mostly due to heart attacks in older people.

Young people are also susceptible to dangers from a heatwave. During every hot spell, the number of drownings rises dramatically, especially among young men. After a lunchtime drink, they decide to cool off with an outdoor swim, but the contrast between their high body temperature and the cold water causes cramp, and they drown. During one heatwave, in the summer of 1989, more than 80 drownings occurred outdoors – over twice the expected rate.

Winter weather, too, brings disease and death in its wake. Once again, elderly people are worst affected, with deaths from hypothermia and related complaints rocketing during prolonged cold spells. The body reacts to cold by closing blood vessels to keep the blood away from the skin and therefore retain heat. However, for old people with poor circulation this can lead to a cycle of falling body temperature, inactivity, a further fall in body temperature and eventually death. In January 1987 the death rate rose by almost 2000 per week largely as a result of hypothermia.

Seasonal reactions to the weather are also common. The best-known is hay fever, actually an allergy to airborne pollen grains. Britain's five million or so sufferers are now helped by

The smog of December 1952 brought London to a halt for a week and left 4000 people dead. It was caused by calm weather creating a layer of warm air over the capital, trapping fumes from coal-fired chimneys. But although smoke is now outlawed in cities, today's invisible pollution is causing other health problems.

anti-histamine drugs, and by the regular daily broadcasts of the pollen count. The condition is at its worst during the early summer, so it particularly affects schoolchildren and students during their exam periods.

Many other long-term health conditions are affected by the weather. Sufferers of rheumatism or arthritis complain they feel worse during changing weather conditions – due to rapid rises and falls in the atmospheric pressure affecting the fluid around their joints. People with chronic lung diseases such as asthma and bronchitis are especially vulnerable to conditions which increase atmospheric pollution. Before the Clean Air Act of 1956, the notorious London smogs killed thousands of people. They would start off as ordinary fog, but the smoke from factories and house fires soon converted this into lethal smog, which would blanket the capital for days on end. The greatest smog of all, in December 1952, left 4000 people dead.

Today, the recent rise in the levels of pollution is causing concern once again. A new form of smog, caused mainly by traffic exhaust emissions, now appears during settled weather conditions in the summer months, leading the television and radio weather forecasters to broadcast an index of air quality together with the traditional pollen count.

MENTAL AND PSYCHOLOGICAL REACTIONS TO THE WEATHER

Biometeorologists have identified another way in which the weather affects our health – the psychological effects. Our state of mind can be radically altered by changes in the weather, especially during heatwaves. When volunteers were tested after being artificially heated up in hot baths, their behaviour changed dramatically. Although their physical reactions were often quicker, they easily became aggressive and argumentative, with unpredictable swings of mood. Other symptoms during hot weather include tiredness, headaches, insomnia, bad temper and forgetfulness.

Productivity drops during hot weather, especially in overheated offices and factories. Getting to and from work can be a problem as well, because the number of traffic accidents actually increases during extremes of heat and sunshine. One theory is that poor weather conditions such as snow and fog make drivers more cautious, whereas in hot weather the body produces chemicals which impair judgement and reduce concentration. Things don't improve when the traffic grinds to a halt, either. During one recent heatwave, the RAC warned motorists against 'homicidal tendencies' when stuck in holiday traffic jams!

Changes in the weather are also known to make serious mental conditions worse. Approaching weather fronts and thunderstorms have long been linked with an increase in mental illnesses such as schizophrenia and manic depression, and the Swiss biometeorologist V Faust suggests that between a third and a half of all suicides are affected by the weather. Levels of street violence and sexual attacks, plus inner-city rioting, all increase during hot weather, although this may simply be a result of more people being out on the streets.

Winter weather has an effect on our mental state, too. During the 1980s, newspapers began to report a newly-discovered condition known as Seasonal Affective Disorder, or SAD. This is a form of clinical depression linked with the lack of sunlight during the winter months, and is said to affect up to half a million people, mostly women, in Britain alone.

FEELING SAD

The memorable initials SAD first hit the headlines in the early 1980s. At first, many people found the idea hard to take seriously – don't we all feel miserable during the cold winter months and happier on a warm summer's day? However, the scientists reassured us that SAD patients were suffering from a genuine medical complaint that was more than just a bout of mid-winter blues.

The problem with diagnosing SAD is that its symptoms - lethargy, sadness, loss of appetite and disturbed sleep - are common to most kinds of clinical depression. Diagnosing whether a particular patient is suffering from SAD, or another form of depression, has proved difficult. For example, it was at first thought that SAD might be linked to the body's secretion of melatonin, the hormone that triggers changes in our seasonal behaviour, but in tests, no differences in melatonin levels were found between SAD patients and others.

SAD has been treated successfully in many cases by exposing the patients to strong artificial light for up to six hours a day during the winter. Yet despite this success, some scientists are still sceptical about the very existence of SAD. An American psychologist, Bill Stiles from Miami University in Ohio, asked depressed patients to record their feelings across the range of seasons. He found there was no significant seasonal variation in the patients' response. His conclusion was that people may be depressed in the winter months but that is because they are already suffering from depression, not because of the weather.

Bill Stiles believes there are two reasons for the emergence of SAD. First, past research always relied on patients remembering their state of mind during previous winters. Most people, he believes, will usually say they felt worse than they actually did. Secondly, the fact that fewer people visit psychiatrists in July than December may simply be due to the fact that, in July, many psychiatrists are on holiday!

Ironically, SAD may just reflect the way we judge ourselves, rather than a true state of mind. As Stiles says, 'One recent survey found that on the average day the average person feels a little bit worse than average'.

LONG-TERM PROBLEMS

Whether or not their problems are truly influenced by the seasons, once those people vulnerable to depression have been identified treatment can often be quick and effective. However, long-term consequences of exposure to the elements are far more worrying. Recent decades have seen a dramatic increase in skin cancers, with cases of the most lethal, melanoma, doubling every ten years. Skin cancer is now the second most common cancer in England and Wales, and looks set to rise. In 1991, a United Nations report predicted that cases worldwide may increase by as many as 300 000 a year – largely because of the partial depletion of the ozone layer.

Skin cancers are caused by exposing the body to the sun's ultra-violet rays – the invisible rays that cause the skin to burn if unprotected. As you'd expect, the effect of these rays increases according to the height and strength of the sun. This is reflected in the increase in the numbers of skin cancers the further south and west in Britain you go. Habitual sun-worshippers are most at risk, but even a single over-exposure to ultra-violet rays can permanently damage the skin.

Fortunately, by using sunscreen creams to protect our skin, we can reduce the risks. We can learn a valuable lesson, too, from those countries where the dangers are even greater. In the Australian state of Queensland, around two-thirds of the population will suffer from skin cancer at some time in their lives. The authorities are so concerned they've begun a campaign to highlight the dangers of sunbathing. A powerful television documentary followed one teenage girl during the last months before her death from skin cancer.

In the United States, too, there's been a move away from the bronzed body-beautiful of the past towards the pale and interesting look typified by Madonna. In California, surfers now plaster themselves in high-factor suncreams and wear bodysuits to reduce their exposure to the sun's harmful rays.

In an attempt to reduce the horrifying death toll from melanoma in Britain – more than 1000 deaths a year at present – the Health Education Authority has run a hard-hitting prevention campaign, using a variety of eye-catching slogans. The message is clear – protect yourself from the sun, or risk an early and painful death.

Ironically, too little sun can be as bad as too much, because sunshine is the catalyst that enables our bodies to make vitamin D, vital for healthy growth. A common Victorian childhood disorder was rickets, which occurred when a lack of vitamin D prevented the bones growing properly. Healthier diets and greater exposure to sunlight have virtually eradicated the disease, although it still occurs in some Asian communities in Britain, where traditional dress designed to protect the body from the harsh sun of the Indian sub-continent prevents sufficient weaker British sunlight reaching the skin.

AND NOW FOR THE GOOD NEWS . . .

It's not all doom and gloom. Just as we've known for centuries that the weather can have adverse effects on our health, so we've known too about its potential benefits. Seaside resorts like Skegness used to advertise their charms as bracing, referring to the supposed healing and rejuvenative powers of the sea air. They were right: the sea air is relatively free from heavy pollution, and rich in sodium and iodine which are vital for the healthy functioning of the heart, liver and kidneys. The seaside climate is also recommended for those suffering from such chronic illnesses as bronchitis and rheumatism.

The idea of recommending different weather conditions for different ailments, which is known as climatotherapy, has a long history. Mountain climates, with their lower levels of water vapour and higher ozone levels, have long been recommended for patients with blood diseases or tuberculosis.

Controlling our exposure to the elements is one way in which we can offset the effects of the weather on our health. Artificial ways of changing local conditions, such as air-conditioning and ionisers, are becoming increasingly common. Good air-conditioning systems can have a dramatic effect on the workers' productivity. However, poorly maintained systems have been blamed for Sick Building Syndrome, in which increased concentrations of germs, bacteria and other pollutants like cigarette smoke cause a wide variety of health complaints.

Despite this catalogue of ways in which the weather can influence our health, a fortunate few people appear immune to its influence. For those people lucky enough not to suffer from sunstroke, hay fever, SAD, migraines, hypothermia or dehydration, there is only one message – when the weather changes, watch the people around you. After all, anyone can be the victim of someone driven to distraction by the weather!

Railway posters, which have since become works of art in their own right, once advertised the health-giving powers of the seaside climate. This one was created by the artist John Hassall in 1909.

Weather and our Wealth

TRIKES, RISES IN INTEREST RATES and unemployment aren't the only factors that influence the British economy. The weather, too, plays its part in determining the economic health of the nation. No one knows how much money is lost because of Britain's weather – the figures are simply too large to calculate – but a glance at an individual industry gives an idea of the problem. Weather-related claims cost the insurance companies an estimated £1 billion every year. One-off events can dwarf even these figures: after the Great Storm of October 1987, claims for damaged roofs, houses and cars topped £1.5 billion.

Later in this chapter we will look at how a Met. Office consultancy, The Weather Initiative, is giving British businesses the help they need to combat the influence of the weather. But first, let's look at the ways in which the weather affects our businesses and commercial organisations.

THE WEATHER AND THE COMMERCIAL WORLD

If you're in business, the weather can cause you problems whatever you grow, make, sell or provide. Farmers are in the front line, especially crop-growers whose entire harvest can be destroyed by a single day's adverse weather. Delicate crops such as fruit and vines are especially vulnerable: in April 1991 a single unseasonal cold snap devastated the hopes of wine-makers in France's most famous vineyards. The frost killed buds on vines in Champagne, Cognac and Bordeaux, wiping out around half the region's wine production in a single night. The damage was estimated at a colossal four billion francs (£400 million).

The weather affects agriculture in more subtle ways, too. Many insect pests rely on favourable winds to carry them to new areas, and crop diseases often depend on damp weather for survival. In the case of potato blight, a kind of fungus, a succession of wet seasons led to the Great Irish Potato Famine of the 1840s, when more than 700 000 people perished.

Transport is also heavily hit by bad weather conditions. During fogs, snow or heavy winds planes are grounded, trains delayed, and roads turned into death-traps. The financial losses can be enormous – through cancelled journeys, delayed freight and in the incalculable number of working hours lost through delays on the way to work.

British Rail seems to suffer more than most. Remember when powdery snow brought British Rail to a grinding halt in February 1991? Despite having invested in the latest snow-clearing equipment, the trains were unable to run. Thousands of frustrated commuters were left stranded, unable to get home. BR's excuse? 'It was the wrong kind of snow . . .'!

For British Rail, these problems aren't new. At 3 p.m. on Monday 9 March 1891, the West Country Express left Paddington on its journey to Plymouth. As it approached the outskirts of London it was stopped in its tracks by the worst blizzard of the nineteenth century. The train finally arrived in Plymouth on Friday 13 March, having spent four days stuck in a snowdrift. The buffet car was closed then, too.

Nor is the rest of the public sector immune to weather problems. During the 1976 drought, water supplies fell to their lowest-ever level, causing reservoirs to run dry. Bans on all but essential water consumption were introduced, and one million people had to use standpipes to collect their water ration. The Government even appointed a Minister for Drought, Denis Howell, on St Swithin's Day!

The energy supply industries suffer from weather problems, too. On one particularly cold February a few years ago electricity consumption reached a peak, with the National

A BR train trapped by a snowdrift near Sittingbourne, Kent, in January 1987.

Grid working flat out. Another surge in consumption might have brought down the whole system. Fortunately, this crisis was averted.

It's not all bad news for the energy industry. Despite the recession hitting company profits, in 1991 British Gas managed to buck the trend by announcing profits up by 46 per cent to a whopping £1.6 billion. One contributor was the cold spell in the early part of 1991, which boosted gas consumption. It's an ill wind . . .

WEATHER AND THE BALANCE SHEET

Some people have always done well out of the British weather. During a heatwave, sales of ice-cream soar; in a cold spell, people buy more warm clothing. Yet it's not just the obvious industries whose sales vary with the weather. A staggering 93 per cent of bread sales are directly related to changes in temperature. Even sales of women's tights, tea and coffee are highly weather-dependent. With many other products, once the 'trigger thresholds' of temperature, sunshine or rainfall are reached, sales patterns change dramatically. Getting the forecast wrong can lead to mountains of unsold goods, as happened to the clothing industry in the cold spring of 1986.

Despite these losses, and the huge commercial potential for saving money, until recently the British industry has taken a fatalistic attitude to weather-related losses. Yet, while it isn't possible to change the weather, it is possible to use accurate forecasting to predict likely buying patterns, and change your commercial strategy accordingly.

THE WEATHER INITIATIVE

The Weather Initiative (TWI) is part of the commercial arm of the Met. Office. It acts as a consultant to retail companies, advising them on how to use the weather to their best advantage. With the right forecasts, businesses can plan ahead to deal with coming conditions. They can predict customer demand, stock the right products at the right time, cut storage costs and target their advertising more carefully. As a result, when the sun does shine, they maximise their profits.

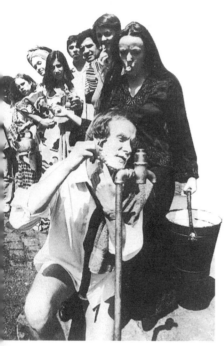

A bathroom in the street? Droughts like the long hot summer of 1976 often exacerbate existing water shortages, leading some water authorities to ration supplies through standpipes in the street.

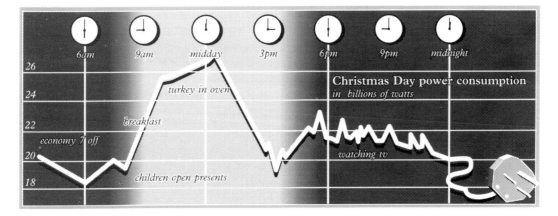

6am 9am midday 3pm 6pm 9pm midnight

26

24

turkey in oven

22

breakfast

Christmas Day power consumption
in billions of watts

economy 7 off

20

watching tv

18

children open presents

TWI give forecasts to companies, usually covering two periods: the first is a detailed forecast for three to ten days in advance, to help them increase or decrease production, or alter their distribution; the other is a forecast for the next ten days to a month, allowing the companies to make long-term plans. However, TWI isn't just about forecasts; expert TWI staff act as consultants to these companies, studying their weather-related problems and suggesting ways of solving them.

TWI have had some notable successes, with clients from all sectors of British business including ICI, Shell UK and Sainsbury's. One major clothing company used TWI data to help plan for seasonal peaks in the sales of T-shirts, a highly weather-dependent product. Normally, the company would buy most T-shirts well before the spring season, sell them during the spring and early summer, and then restock with their warmer autumn clothes in August. However, during the summer of 1990 TWI data forecast a warm spell during late August, by which time the T-shirts are usually sold out. So the company made a bulk purchase of T-shirts, delayed their autumn collection and awaited the heatwave. The last two weeks of August were sunny and warm and the company did a roaring trade. The bottom line was an increase in profits of almost £1 million, at a cost of just £50 000!

On a shorter time-scale, food manufacturers and caterers can be left with mountains of unsold food if the weather

The demand for electricity on an average Christmas Day climbs steadily during the morning, then drops sharply in the afternoon – presumably when most of the nation are doing the washing up or going for a walk. The electricity consumption is much greater during those elusive white Christmases.

conditions change. One group of motorway caterers discovered that for every degree the temperature rose above 20°C (68°F), they lost a staggering £70 000 worth of sales in hot meals every day! After calling in TWI, they used advance forecasts to plan stock changes. When good weather was expected, they increased the number of salads and cold foods on sale; in poor weather, they provided hot meals.

In the two years since TWI was set up, its turnover has grown to over £600 000 a year, the profits from which are ploughed back into the Met. Office. Yet the real benefit is to the companies themselves. Estimates suggest that savings can amount to around one-tenth of a per cent of a company's annual turnover. It may not sound much, but across British industry as a whole, the savings could add up to hundreds of millions of pounds. So far, the Met. Office scheme is the only one of its kind in the world.

WEATHER AND THE STOCK EXCHANGE

There have been many attempts to link the rises and falls in the Stock Exchange Index with the weather: sunspots, 11-year cycles and changes in atmospheric pressure have all been put forward as possibilities. Indeed, the infamous Black Monday, when the Stock Exchange saw its greatest ever one-day fall and the start of the 1987 Crash, occurred just three days after the Great Storm. Some journalists even linked the two events and predicted Armageddon!

The truth is that the Stock Exchange Index is affected by so many variables – interest rates, elections, unemployment figures – that the weather is unlikely to play more than an insignificant part in determining its rise or fall.

However, individual sectors can be affected by the weather. As we've seen, the most vulnerable in recent years have been the insurance companies, many of which reported their first ever annual losses after the devastation wreaked by the storm in October 1987. Since then, things have gone from bad to worse. The series of storms that hit the United Kingdom in January 1990 caused the world's largest ever insurance losses, with an estimated cost to the companies of more than

Facing page Bad weather can spell disaster for insurance companies. Claims for damage after the storms of early 1990 ran into billions of pounds, leading to higher premiums for householders.

£5 billion – equivalent to £100 for every man, woman and child in the country. The companies have also been badly hit by weather problems further afield, such as Hurricane Hugo, which devastated much of the southern United States.

Long-term climatic change has affected the insurance industry, too. Unless the rainfall in south-east England and East Anglia improves dramatically in the next year or two, companies face big payouts. Years of persistent drought have caused a fall in the water table, which has dried out the clay soil around the foundations of many houses. As a result, claims for subsidence have rocketed, from an annual average of £100–£150 million during the 1980s to more than £400 million in the first nine months of 1991. There is a knock-on effect on premiums, and in the long-term Dr Julian Ferrand, the Insurance Ombudsman, foresees that insurance companies may soon find it cheaper to 'write off' a house damaged by subsidence than repair it.

WEATHER AND THE COMMODITIES MARKET

There is one City institution that is greatly affected by the weather, however. The London Futures and Options Exchange (known as Fox) deals in buying and selling contracts to deliver such commodities as coffee, tea or wheat. However, with the exception of that drunk by the frantic brokers, the actual coffee is never seen by those who buy and sell it. That's because the market works on a 'futures' basis – traders buy and sell the right to purchase or sell a certain amount of the commodity within a set time, at a particular price. For example, one trader might agree to buy 50 tonnes of Brazilian coffee beans at $878 per tonne in 90 days. He is gambling on the belief that the price will rise in the meantime, so that at the end of the period (or indeed any time between now and then) he can sell on the right to buy at a higher price.

The weather conditions affecting the market are in the future – at the time the contract will end. For example, supposing the weather in Brazil is wet and windy, the coffee crop may be partly destroyed. If that's the case, there'll be a shortfall and the price of Brazilian coffee will rise. If the opposite is the case, and good weather produces a bumper crop, prices will fall accordingly.

So long-term forecasting, never very reliable at the best of times, is the key. If one trader can gain access to a more accurate forecast, and more importantly if he can keep it secret, he may be able to go against market predictions and make a killing. If the forecast turns out to be wrong, of course, he may become bankrupt.

WEATHER AND POLITICS

Traditionally, politics is not seen as a weather-related activity. However, it has often been said that the Conservatives hope for wet weather on General Election Day as this is supposed to keep Labour voters away from the polls. In the past, this may have been true, because until relatively recently Labour voters were less likely to have cars and so would be reluctant to walk to the polling stations in bad weather!

The last recorded instance when bad weather may have contributed to election defeat was in 1970. Prime Minister Harold Wilson called the election in May, when England looked set for the semi-finals of the soccer World Cup and the weather forecasters predicted a flaming June. Wilson hoped the 'feelgood factor', reinforced by the sunshine, would return him to government. However, after a fine start to the month, thunderstorms swept across the country, the English lost 3–2 to West Germany and the Conservatives romped home with a majority of 31 seats. Four years later Harold Wilson got his revenge when, after the miseries of the three-day-week, power cuts and freezing February weather, the British people had had enough and voted him back into power.

In contrast, the General Election of April 1992 fell on the warmest day of the year so far, with only the outlying constituency of the Western Isles suffering any rain. Yet contrary to the theory that good weather brings out more Labour voters, the Conservatives scored an easy victory. In the words of Anthony King, Professor of Politics at the University of Essex, 'It looks as though if people are determined to vote they will vote, come rain or shine'.

Jolly voting weather – the General Election of April 1992 took place during a spell of unseasonably warm weather, but did it affect the result?

Weather and the Past

T HE CLIMATE IN BRITAIN has never stood still, and its fluctuations have had many dramatic impacts on our history. It has changed the course of battles, changed the fortunes of empires, caused spectacular disasters and, in some cases, made history itself. Although official weather records only go back two or three centuries, the evidence from scientists, historians and writers goes back much further.

Seven thousand years ago the ice sheets of the last great ice age retreated as temperatures rose. The improved climate helped cavemen turn from hunting to farming, with populations in prehistoric Europe increasing until a cold period set in about 2500 BC. Conditions later improved around 500 BC, and this warmer period coincided, as with many other examples of colonial expansion, with the spread of the Roman Empire.

BATTLING WITH THE WEATHER

The best accounts of historical weather are those given at the time of our most famous battles. It's no exaggeration to say that the British owe much of their historical success to the help given by unpredictable weather. Julius Caesar may have come, seen and conquered – but not at his first attempt. In 55 BC his first invasion was stopped by strong north-westerly winds. Of course, he succeeded eventually and the Romans introduced the grapevine to England during this warm time.

But by about AD 400 conditions deteriorated again, as the climate in Britain and the rest of Europe grew increasingly wet and cold. Around this time the Roman Empire went into slow decline, while drought in the heart of Eurasia sent Barbarian hordes and refugees into Europe, further unsettling the Roman Empire. For the next 600 years (the so-called Dark Ages) glaciers in northern Europe grew larger in the bitter winters, and a small ice age set in. Not until the 1100s did conditions improve again, and summers grew so warm in Britain that vines were grown as far north as the Pennines.

The climatic pendulum swung back again at the start of the thirteenth century, when violent storms in the North Sea killed hundreds of thousands of people along the British and Continental coasts, and towns like Dunwich on the Suffolk coast were so severely flooded they sank into the sea. As summers grew wetter and winters colder, harvests failed, leading to widespread famine. Hamlets were abandoned in many areas as farming deteriorated.

But the weather rescued the British against the French at Crécy (1346) and Agincourt (1415) during the Hundred Years' War. At Crécy, a storm that had been raging cleared and the sun shone directly into the eyes of the French army. At Agincourt, constant rain had turned the ground into a mud-bath in which the French horses got stuck. This, together with the technical superiority of the English bowmen, allowed the much smaller English forces to triumph.

The climate steadily deteriorated into what was known as the Little Ice Age, from 1550–1750, when winters were so cold that the River Thames froze over in London and frost fairs were held on it. The worst storm in recorded history in 1703 is thought to have killed 10 000 people (see pages 16–17). Scotland was very badly hit by a series of failed harvests, and the famines there are thought to have killed more people than the Black Death (which killed 1.4 million people), leading to mass emigration to Ulster and a collapse in the economy which hastened the Act of Union with England in 1707.

As the climate steadily recovered, odd periods of bad weather cropped up. Charles Dickens wrote about the hard winters and white Christmases at the turn of the nineteenth century, and J M Turner painted spectacularly red sunsets.

The winter of 1813–14 saw the last of the frost fairs to be held on the frozen River Thames. Bonfires were lit on the ice, entertainments were performed, and thousands of visitors enjoyed the spectacle. Fairs like this were common during the Little Ice Age, when the climate turned cold for two centuries.

The British capture the French guns at Waterloo, in 1815. Bad weather delayed Napoleon's attack, and may have lost him the battle. Victor Hugo wrote 'A few drops of water, an unseasonable cloud crossing the sky, sufficed for the overthrow of a world'.

Both of these weather conditions were caused by a global veil of dust spewed out from volcanic eruptions which blocked the sunlight and cooled the earth.

In 1815 the weather turned another historical battle into a British victory at Waterloo and changed the course of history. Napoleon delayed his attack because of torrential rain, hoping for an improvement in the weather. When none came he finally gave orders to advance, but his delay gave the Allied generals, led by Wellington, just enough time to rally their forces, and Napoleon and his great army were defeated. He was unlucky with the weather, too, when he attempted to invade Russia. Like Hitler more than a century later, he was forced back by the Russians' greatest military asset, 'General Winter'. Temperatures rose again in the 1820s until more wet weather hit Europe in the 1840s, leading to the Potato Famine in Ireland, in which half the population died of starvation.

The weather for the latter half of the nineteenth century was exceptionally variable, and had a profound effect on agriculture. From 1876 to 1882 there was a disastrous run of wet summers, which produced bad wheat harvests. Together with the importation of cheap wheat from America, this was enough to send British agriculture into a tailspin from which it barely recovered until the Second World War. As with most economic and social changes that are driven by climate, the agricultural depression resulted in large-scale human migrations to Australia and North America.

The climate improved markedly in the twentieth century, and meanwhile the weather again played an important part in the history of Britain. At Dunkirk, as the German forces pushed the Allies back on to the beaches, a pea-soup fog blanketed the Channel with absolutely calm seas. This enabled the famous flotilla of tiny boats to rescue 300 000 men without exposing them to German air attack.

Perhaps the most critical battle weather came towards the end of the war, as Britain and the other Allies prepared for D-Day, the invasion of Normandy to liberate France. The invasion, the largest then known in history, was entirely dependent on the right weather conditions.

A look at the historical records suggested the month of June, so plans were made for invasion in early June 1944. On 4 June, as the troops waited, the weather worsened, delaying the invasion. General Eisenhower was faced with a tough decision. If he decided not to go ahead, the invasion might be delayed by a whole year; but if he did go ahead and the weather was bad, it might prove a fiasco. Just as he was making up his mind, a new forecast suggested a 'gap' of good weather, so the invasion went ahead. Ironically, the German forecasters predicted the weather would prevent a successful invasion, so many officers were on leave and troops were engaged elsewhere.

Historical landmarks apart, there has been a marked warming from the early twentieth century onwards, although interspersed with the intermittent cold spells. Is this another swing of the climatic pendulum or are we heading into a man-made disaster: the greenhouse effect? The last chapter of the book examines whether the greenhouse effect is real and what other lessons we can learn from history.

The Normandy landings, D-Day, 6 June 1944. The Allied invasion went ahead during a spell of good weather which was vital for success. The Allies needed calm seas for naval support, good visibility with little cloud cover for the Air Force, and low wind speeds for the parachutists.

GREAT WEATHER EVENTS

The weather has played a part in our history in its own right, too, as the following table shows.

55 BC Julius Caesar was thwarted in his first invasion of Britain because of strong north-westerly winds.

August–September 1588 The Spanish Armada was wrecked during its retreat past Scotland and Ireland.

2–6 September 1666 Following a prolonged dry spell, the Great Fire of London was made more devastating by a strong easterly wind which fanned the flames.

26–27 November 1703 The Great Storm, thought to be Britain's worst ever. Towns were devastated, Eddystone Lighthouse was destroyed and Daniel Defoe counted 17 000 trees down in Kent alone.

Winter 1813–14 The last of the Thames frost fairs took place on the ice-covered river.

27 December 1836 An avalanche of snow killed eight people at Lewes, Sussex.

22 July 1858 During a heatwave the temperature at Tonbridge in Kent was recorded at 38°C (100.5°F), Britain's unofficial highest ever recorded temperature.

25 October 1859 The ship *Royal Charter* was wrecked off the North Welsh coast in a severe storm. Almost 500 people died.

28 December 1879 A train and 75 passengers were lost when the Tay Bridge was destroyed during a storm.

26 January 1884 Pressure fell to 926.5 millibars in Perthshire – the lowest ever recorded in Britain.

15 May 1893 Britain's longest ever drought in a single place ended, after 73 days without rain in East London.

11 February 1895 The equal lowest air temperature was recorded in Britain: −27.2°C (−17°F), in Braemar, Scotland (see also 10 January 1982).

31 January 1902 Pressure rose to 1055 millibars in Aberdeen – the highest ever recorded in Britain.

13–15 June 1903 Britain's longest period of continuous rain – it fell for 58 hours.

22 July 1907 Hailstones 'the size of hens' eggs' fell in South Wales.

9–10 July 1923 In a massive thunderstorm, 6924 flashes of lightning were recorded in 6 hours over London.

23 August 1935 5.1 mm (0.2 in) of rain fell in one minute at Croydon Airport, Surrey – the highest ever 'extreme of point' rainfall.

28 July 1948 The warmest night ever recorded in Britain: 23°C (73.4°F) in London.

15 August 1952 Over 228 mm (9 in) of rain fell in a few hours, flooding the North Devon town of Lynmouth.

5–9 December 1952 The 'Great Smog of London', in which more than 4000 people died.

31 January–1 February 1953 East coast storms flooded low-lying parts of East Anglia. Over 300 people were killed, and thousands were made homeless.

18 July 1955 Britain's highest ever rainfall in 24 hours – 279 mm (11 in) of rain fell in Martinstown, Dorset.

Winter 1962–3 The coldest since at least 1795; on 6–7 February snow fell continuously for 36 hours.

25 December 1970 The last official white Christmas in London.

9 May 1973 Greatest recorded temperature range: from −7°C (19°F) before dawn, to 22°C (71.6°F) in the afternoon in Tayside, Scotland.

2 June 1975 Snow fell across the Midlands and south-east England, preventing cricket at Buxton in the Peak District.

Summer 1976 The great drought. In southern England, no rain fell for between 35 and 42 days, up to 29 August.

1–6 and 2–7 July 1976 The only recorded instance of six consecutive days on which the temperature reached 90°F (32.2°C), in Gloucestershire and Sussex.

14 August 1979 A storm devastated the Fastnet Yacht Race off the south-west approaches: 19 yachts sank, with the loss of 15 lives.

10 January 1982 The equal lowest air temperature recorded in Britain: −27.2°C (−17°F) at Braemar in Scotland (see also 11 February 1895).

20 March 1986 The highest recorded wind speed in the British Isles: a gust of 278 kph (173 mph) in the Cairngorms.

16 October 1987 The Great Storm hit southern England in the early hours; 19 people died in the worst storm since 1703.

25 January 1990 'Burns Day Storm' left 46 people dead across Britain; *'Allo, 'allo!* star Gorden Kaye was seriously injured.

26 February 1990 High winds combined with high tides to breach the sea wall at Towyn, North Wales, flooding the town. Hundreds of people lost their homes to the floodwaters.

3 August 1990 The highest air temperature officially recorded in Britain: 37.1°C (98.8°F) at Cheltenham in Gloucestershire.

1990 Globally, the warmest year ever.

1991 Globally, the second warmest year ever.

The Future

YOUR DAILY WEATHER FORECAST for the next 24 hours is pretty accurate but, beyond the next five days, forecasting is an unreliable science. There has always been a need for long-range predictions, for planning warfare to agriculture and industry, yet long-term weather forecasting has been the Holy Grail of meteorology.

One of the biggest blunders in long-range prediction took place during the Second World War. The German attack on Moscow in October 1941 depended entirely on mild weather but the meteorological predictions were disastrous. Even though the German army was well aware of the severity of a Russian winter, they relied totally on the advice of the German weather service under Franz Baur. He had predicted a mild winter based on statistical probability: the previous two winters had been severe over Northern Europe, so he reckoned a third successive severe winter was highly unlikely. However, the winter of 1941–2 broke all records for its severity, with temperatures around Moscow probably colder than at any time for the previous 250 years, plunging to a low of −40°C (−40°F). The German advance was decimated: the troops suffered frostbite, machinery shattered and supplies stopped. Yet even in the face of total defeat, Baur still remained confident that his forecast was accurate. How much his failure contributed to the eventual downfall of the invasion of Russia – and arguably the outcome of the war – is still debatable, but it has had a sobering effect on all long-range forecasters ever since.

THE THEORY OF SUNSPOTS

What forecasters have desperately sought is some sort of constant cycle of events on which to base their predictions. The idea of cycles of weather is nothing new: the seven years of plenty and seven years of drought in the Bible is just one example. The best hopes have long been pinned on the theory that ice ages and warmer periods are due to slow changes in the earth's orbit around the sun. This satisfactorily explains climate changes on the very long time-scale – from thousands to millions of years. Very much second best is the 11-year cycle in sunspots. The Chinese were the first to notice these dark spots on the surface of the sun – dust storms left the sky so dark that they were able to look directly at the sun during the day and record the larger spots. They've been recording sunspots ever since for over 2000 years and so have provided a marvellous historical record.

Scientists grew particularly excited when they found the same sort of 11-year cycle in other places. Botanists studying tree rings found they had an 11-year cycle which shows an annual historical record of weather – generally speaking, the larger the ring the milder the weather. Scientists grew even more excited when they found some notable exceptions to this tree ring cycle during the years 1645 to 1715. This 70-year period is known as the Little Ice Age (see Weather and the Past) because of its severe cold, and it correlated with the Chinese records, which showed sunspots were less common during this period.

So were the earth's ice ages due to a lack of sunspot activity? Meteorologists have searched in vain for convincing evidence that sunspots really do influence the weather. They've hunted high and low through past records to find changes in weather every 11 years, but without totally convincing success. What seems to work well in one place at one time doesn't work somewhere else or at a later time: fluctuations in the weather in phase with sunspots can be thrown off-course elsewhere in the weather system, making them less reliable than we thought.

What we should be asking instead is how sunspots could affect our weather? One thing we do know is that the sun's heat is not involved because it has the uncanny knack of always staying constant, no matter what the sunspot activity. We know that giant flares on the surface of the sun spew out storms of ions into space. They soak into the earth's upper atmosphere and produce the northern lights (the aurora borealis). It's possible that the ions in the upper atmosphere affect our weather. An old Scottish saying, 'The first great aurora of the autumn is followed by a storm in two days', recognises that strong auroras signal bad weather. And scientists have recently found evidence that a severe aurora deepens depressions in the Gulf of Alaska and so strengthens the storm systems that later strike North America.

The solar flares could be altering our weather by changing the chemistry of the upper atmosphere. The trouble is that, despite the best computers available, we still don't have a computer model advanced enough to simulate the effects of the sunspot-driven winds in the upper atmosphere, let alone the changes in chemistry that might accompany them. Perhaps most frustrating of all, it can take decades or even hundreds of years of recordings before you can prove your long-term forecasting system works.

To complicate matters even further, there could be other cycles at work as well as the sunspots. The record of temperatures in central England for the past 300 years, droughts in central and western United States over four centuries, ice core records from Greenland and the global record of temperatures at sea established from 1850 all hint at a regular cycle of about 20 years. This could be due to an 18.6 year cycle in the tidal effects of the moon, or the doubling of the sunspot cycle to 22 years, when the sun's magnetic field reverses after each 11-year sunspot cycle. How this could affect the earth's weather no one knows. Chemical analysis of tree rings reveals a cycle of solar activity of 420 years, but unfortunately we have no historical records with which to compare this cycle!

Another recently discovered factor is the sea current, which scientists believe is the reason for Britain's mild and muggy climate. They have demonstrated that a sea movement called the Agulhas current carries warm water from the Pacific and

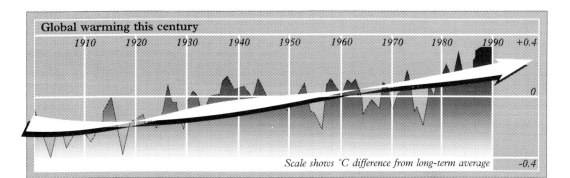

Global warming this century

1910 1920 1930 1940 1950 1960 1970 1980 1990 +0.4

0

Scale shows °C difference from long-term average -0.4

Indian Oceans, round South Africa to the Atlantic and into the northern hemisphere. It takes up to three years for this heat to be transported to the North Atlantic, so measuring the temperatures of the current could help to predict future weather.

The fact is that fluctuations in the seasons from year to year reflect the immense complexity of the global climate. We are making progress in understanding how the various components are interconnected, and satellite measurements in particular are providing an increasingly detailed picture of how the global climate varies from year to year. It may be that expanding information will produce improved forecasting rules. Equally, they might do no more than confirm a never-ending variety of seemingly random patterns. So we may never be able to make accurate forecasts of the coming seasons, an ability that has become increasingly important if we are to discover more about the greenhouse effect.

The temperature is rising. Average global temperatures have risen about 0.5°C (0.9°F) this century, but will we fry in the 21st century?

THE FUTURE: FREEZE OR FRY?

What is happening to the weather? From one year to the next our weather records are being broken: drought, heatwaves, storms, cold winters, wet summers (see page 13). The warnings are that we're heading for an Apocalyptic global warming, due to an increase in the greenhouse effect. Yet not so long ago the fear was that we were plunging into another ice age, sparked by a series of bitter winters in the 1970s. What are we to make of it all?

It's hardly surprising you're confused, although many scientists agree about the greenhouse effect. Put simply, the earth is getting warmer because we've polluted it with gases that trap heat. The phenomenon is called the greenhouse effect because these gases behave like the glass in a greenhouse, letting in the sun's heat but preventing it escaping. Heat is re-radiated back off the earth's surface, but the greenhouse gases trap it. Strangely enough, we need a balanced amount of greenhouse gases in order to survive – if we removed them all the earth would drop into another ice age.

It doesn't sound much to say that the world might heat up by between 0.3–0.5°C (0.5–0.9°F) but that extra warmth is enough to expand the oceans, melt substantial chunks of the polar ice sheets, pushing the levels of the world's oceans higher, triggering ecological catastrophe and leading to starvation and civil strife. These are seen as the inevitable consequences of human activity increasing the greenhouse effect.

Unfortunately, the climate is so complicated it's very difficult to be sure if the earth is getting warmer because of the greenhouse effect or something else. There are a bewildering number of twists and turns to this story. So here are the facts as we know them now. The average climate of the world has been growing steadily warmer for the past 80 years. The past decade has been exceptionally warm (the seven warmest years since 1860 have occurred between 1980 and 1991 and the two warmest were 1990 and 1991). As a result, the sea water is expanding, glaciers and ice caps are melting and making the level of the seas rise. The levels of polluting gases – carbon dioxide, methane, nitrous oxides and others – thought to cause the greenhouse effect are increasing. The finger of blame points to all sorts of culprits: power stations running on fossil fuels spew out carbon dioxide; burning straw stubble or forests produces carbon dioxide and nitrous oxides; farmyard animals and rice fields make methane; and our beloved cars churn out clouds of carbon dioxide and nitrous oxides.

But that's all we are able to say for certain. Scientists disagree on how, when and by how much the earth will warm. Part of the problem is that so many other factors are involved

On 7 May 1976 the temperature in London reached 24.4°C (82°F), the hottest day in early May for a decade. The rest of that summer was the hottest and driest on record – but was it a natural phenomenon or caused by man-made pollution?

as well. For instance, the polluting sulphur, which is belched out from many power stations and causes acid rain, could also by a strange twist of fate be saving us from the greenhouse warming. Each microscopic particle of sulphur floating in the air helps to block out sunshine, so dirty sulphur may actually be keeping us cool!

There are also the clouds to be considered. As the earth gets warmer, more water will evaporate from the seas to make more clouds. Because clouds block out sunshine before it reaches the earth's surface, they'll cool down the earth. But clouds also block heat escaping from the earth, slowing down the cooling process. It is not an easily-solved problem. The clouds are also getting thicker thanks to the sulphur pollution.

Although figures show the climate is becoming warmer, even that idea could be misleading. It's the night-time temperatures that are getting significantly warmer, probably because the larger numbers of clouds are insulating the night sky like a blanket. Of course, there are also natural variations in the climate that we are still very unsure about (as discussed in the previous section).

So you see, the greenhouse effect is far from a simple picture. Nevertheless, it must be taken seriously because the omens look serious, and the consequences of gambling against it ever happening are so dire we cannot afford to take the risk.

How will we be affected?

One way in which scientists are trying to predict what will happen to us in the greenhouse future is by looking back at ancient history to find patterns that could be applied to the years ahead. By collecting fossils and ancient pollen from three million years ago, they have found the earth was then 3 to 4° C (about 5 to 7° F) warmer than now, with forests growing as far north as the Arctic coast of Greenland, and the warmer seas up to 35 metres (115 feet) higher than current levels.

How does that compare to today? The sea level is already rising by 2 mm (1/12 in) per year, and at the same time southern England is tilting downwards at a rate of about 4 mm (1/6 in) a year. The sea level might eventually rise by

We could be in for big problems if global warming really sets in. Sea levels are already thought to be rising and, together with more storms like the ones of 1987 and 1990, we risk terrible flooding in places less than 5 metres (16 feet) above sea level. Yet the lessons of the 1953 flood of the eastern counties haven't been learnt. Sea defences are in a poor condition and, even though the Thames Flood Barrier was built to protect London in case of flooding, it may prove inadequate in the future.

Land below the
5 metre contour

50–355 cm (20–140 in), easily topping our sea defences and seriously flooding low-lying coastal areas, deltas, estuaries and river systems. Insurance companies are re-assessing the risk of coastal flooding due to climate changes and may charge extra premiums to thousands of businesses with factories and offices less than 5 metres (16 feet) above sea level. Vast areas of East Anglia and sizeable chunks elsewhere in Britain fall below that line, some of them 50 km (30 miles) inland from existing sea defences. Farming has made the situation far worse. Draining the Fens, for example, has caused the land to shrink and become lower by 2–3 metres (6–9 feet).

Yet the greenhouse effect could be very good for some plants. Extra carbon dioxide stimulates the growth of plants by boosting their photosynthesis (by which they make their food), and also helps to cut down their water demands. So plants of the greenhouse world will grow more rapidly with less watering. The warmer nights will also lengthen the growing season.

Unfortunately, not all the benefits of the greenhouse effect will produce better crop yields. Weeds will also benefit from the extra carbon dioxide, while not all crop plants can use the additional gas. The warmer temperatures might also lead to an explosion in crop diseases and bugs, just as the mild winter of 1988–9 brought on a plague of greenfly and their accompanying virus diseases the following spring. So we have to be careful before rushing to conclusions that the greenhouse effect could be good for crops.

The story for wild plants will be even more bewildering. Natural plants have adapted to their environments over hundreds and thousands of years. The sudden lurch into warmer climates could have catastrophic effects, with delicate flora such as alpine plants coming into flower early because of the warm springs. Bees might miss the early flowering, and without pollination some plants will face extinction.

What will life be like in Britain? Some say that within 20 years the summers might be as hot and dry as those in the south of France, but others disagree and either say there will be no noticeable change, or that we will have extreme fluctuations in our local climate.

Our climate is already becoming very erratic. The heatwave of 1976 has parallels in the first half of the eighteenth century during the Little Ice Age. Wild fluctuations in heat were a feature of that period, both at the beginning of that time when temperatures fell and at the end when temperatures recovered again, with interludes of great heat interspersed with record cold spells. There were also frequent famines in Africa, as there are today.

Alongside all these uncertainties one of the most alarming prospects is a sudden catastrophic change which could turn all the predictions upside down. The big nightmare is what might happen to the ocean currents. Many parts of the world depend on the quirks of these currents for their climate: Britain and the rest of north-west Europe generally have fairly mild winters because of the enormous amount of heat released by the Gulf Stream. Less well-known is the 'Atlantic conveyor': every winter, relatively salty water rises at about the latitude of

The promenade at Cannes, in the South of France. Will our British climate turn Mediterranean, with palm trees growing in Glasgow in years to come?

Iceland as winds sweep the surface. Exposed to the cool air, the salty water releases heat and then sinks to the bottom again. The heat given off is equal to 30 per cent of the yearly input of the sun's energy to the North Atlantic. Studies of the last ice age suggest that this current may be particularly vulnerable to small changes in the salinity and temperature of the sea. If the current failed we could end up substantially cooler instead of warmer. What a paradox!

So is the end of our civilisation nigh? The prospect of the greenhouse effect warming the globe slightly over the next few decades is sometimes dismissed as unimportant compared with natural fluctuations of temperature from season to season and even from day to day. Yet changes in temperature of one or two degrees, no bigger than the ones we are likely to experience over the next 20 years, have had profound influences on human cultures over the past 2000 years.

Professor Hubert Lamb at the University of East Anglia has found that changes in climate coincided with major upheavals in past civilisations. For example, the spreading influences of Buddha (who died in 483 BC) and Confucius (who died in 479 BC), with their acceptance of suffering, both coincided with a long period of extreme cold in China up to 200 BC.

As we saw in Weather and the Past, periods of adverse climate can trigger famines such as the medieval starvations, produce mass migrations like the Scots' colonisation of Ireland, lead to the collapse of civilisations such as the Roman Empire and spark off wars. Perhaps the most succinct lesson we can learn about failing to adapt to a changing climate comes from the Vikings. They were encouraged to colonise Greenland during a period of mild weather and the accompanying retreat of North Sea ice in the ninth and tenth centuries. During the thirteenth and fourteenth centuries, however, temperatures dropped by about 2°C (3.6°F) and the Norse colonists were completely wiped out because they failed to adapt to the colder weather.

The lessons of the past are stark: adapt or die. Alternatively we must find ways of controlling the greenhouse effect, if indeed it is already upon us.

ACKNOWLEDGEMENTS

This book would not have been possible without the help and expertise of the staff of the Met. Office at Bracknell. We would especially like to thank Gordon Higgins for his initial encouragement, and Barry Parker for co-ordinating the whole project. Bob Riddaway provided useful comments, Maurice Tall compiled data on weather records and Peter Woolford in the Library pointed us in the direction of some fascinating literature on the weather.

The staff of the BBC Reference Library, especially the Subject Specialists, used their expertise to unearth many fascinating reports, articles and snippets of information.

The wonderful support of Sharon Ward in our BBC office proved invaluable, as she kept us organised and serviced.

Professor Hubert Lamb of the University of East Anglia gave us the benefit of his enormous expertise on the history of climate change, covered in Chapter 11.

Much of the information in the chapters on Extremes and Freaks was provided by the Tornado and Storm Research Organisation (TORRO). Founded in 1974, this is a private research group that collects information on weird weather phenomena. They are interested in hearing from anyone who has witnessed such unusual events as tornadoes, waterspouts, ball lightning or showers of unusual objects. TORRO can be contacted by writing to Michael Rowe and Terence Meaden, 21 Bankview, Buckland Park, Lymington, Hants SO41 8YG.

PICTURE CREDITS

BBC Books would like to thank the following for providing photographs, and for permission, to reproduce copyright material. While every effort has been made to trace and acknowledge all copyright holders, we would like to apologise should there have been any errors or omissions:

Black and white photographs and illustrations
11 above David Killpatrick, left Camera Press; 12 Tony Garrett; 13 Tony Garrett; 15 FLPA; 17 Camera Press; 19 Tony Garrett; 20 Popperfoto; 21 Tony Garrett; 23 Topham; 24 Topham; 25 Tony Garrett; 27 Camera Press; 28 BBC; 29 Hulton Picture Company; 31 Fortean Picture Library; 32 Fortean Picture Library; 35 Tony Garrett; 36 Colin Andrews/The Met. Office; 39 top Tony Garrett, bottom Crown Copyright; 40 Tony Garrett; 41 The University of Dundee; 42–43 Tony Garrett; 45 Tony Garrett; 47 top John Frost Historical Newspaper Services, bottom Tony Garrett; 48 Crown Copyright; 49 BP Educational Services; 50 BBC; 51 Crown Copyright; 53 below J F P Galvin/The Met. Office, middle Crown Copyright, bottom Crown Copyright; 55 Crown Copyright; 56 Crown Copyright; 59 Topham; 62 top FLPA, bottom FLPA; 63 Hulton Picture Company; 69 top D N Dalton/NHPA, bottom FLPA; 70 top FLPA, bottom FLPA; 71 FLPA; 72 FLPA; 73 left Nature Photographers Ltd, Andrew Cleave, above FLPA; 74 FLPA, 80 Camera Press; 85 National Railway Museum; 87 Topham; 88 Popperfoto; 89 Tony Garrett; 91 Emma Lee/TRIP; 93 Topham; 95 The Mansell Collection; 96 The Mansell Collection; 97 Camera Press; 103 Tony Garrett; 104 Hulton Picture Company; 107 Hulton Picture Company.

Colour section
1 FLPA; 2 FLPA; 3FLPA; 4–5 above FLPA, right FLPA; 6–7 above Nature Photographers Ltd, left FLPA; 8 FLPA; 9 above Nature Photographers Ltd, left FLPA; 10 FLPA; 11 Helen Rogers/TRIP; 12–13 FLPA; 14–15 above Science Photo Library; right Science Photo Library; 16 FLPA.

FURTHER READING

GENERAL

DAVID BOWEN, *Britain's Weather: its Workings, Lore and Forecasting* (David & Charles 1969)

W J BURROUGHS, *Watching the World's Weather* (Cambridge University Press 1991)

DEREK ELSOM, *Earth* (Simon & Schuster 1992)

DICK FILE, *Weather Watch* (Fourth Estate 1990)

BILL GILES, *The Story of Weather* (HMSO 1990)

INGRID HOLFORD, *The Guinness Book of Weather Facts and Feats* (Guinness Superlatives 1977)

G LOCKHART, *The Weather Companion* (Wiley 1988)

M QUIN, *Weather in Focus* (F Watts 1990)

FRANCIS WILSON, *The Great British Obsession* (Jarrold 1990)

WEATHER LORE

MAVIS BUDD, *Weather Wisdom* (Piatkus Books 1986)

DAVID BOWEN, *Weather Lore for Gardeners* (Thorsons 1978)

WILLIAM FOGGITT, *William Foggitt's Weather Book* (Countryside Publications Ltd 1978)

PAUL JOHN GOLDSACK, *Weatherwise* (David & Charles 1986)

ALBERT LEE, *Weather Wisdom* (Congdon & Weed 1976)

RON LOBECK, *Weather Wisdom, Fact or Fiction?* (Geerings of Ashford 1989)

PAUL J MARRIOTT, *Red Sky at Night, Shepherd's Delight* (Sheba Books 1981)

ROBIN PAGE, *Weather Forecasting the Country Way* (Penguin Books 1981)

WEATHER AND OUR DAILY LIVES

W J MAUNDER, *The Value of the Weather* (Electricity Supply Authority Engineering Institute 1970)

ALLEN AND VIVIEN PERRY, *Climate and Society* (Bell & Hyman 1986)

FELIX GAD SULMAN, *Health, Weather and Climate* (S Karger 1976)

WEATHER AND NATURAL HISTORY

NORMAN ELKINS, *Weather and Bird Behaviour* (P & A D Poyser 1983)

WEIRD WEATHER

J ERICKSON, *Violent Storms* (TAB Books 1988)

G J MCEWAN, *Freak Weather* (Robert Hale 1991)

G T MEADEN, *The Stonehenge Solution* (Souvenir Press 1992)

WEATHER AND THE PAST

H H LAMB, *Climate, History and the Modern World* (Methuen 1982)

OUR FUTURE WEATHER

JOHN GRIBBIN, *Future Weather* (Penguin Books 1982)

JOHN GRIBBIN, *Hothouse Earth: the Greenhouse Effect and Gaia* (Bantam Press 1990)

JOHN GRIBBIN, *Forecasts, Famines and Freezes* (Wildwood House 1976)

ARTICLES ON THE WEATHER

W J BURROUGHS, *'Cold comfort in the crystal ball'*, New Scientist, 5 January 1991.

DEREK ELSOM, *'Catch a falling frog'*, New Scientist, 2 June 1988.

DEREK ELSOM, *'Learn to live with lightning'*, New Scientist, 24 June 1989.

JOHN GRIBBIN, *'Inside science: climate now'*, New Scientist, 16 March 1991.

JOHN AND MARY GRIBBIN, *'Climate and history: the Westvikings' saga'*, New Scientist, 20 January 1990.

INDEX

Page numbers in italics refer to illustrations